Rhonda Winfield

WHEN JOHNNY DOESN'T COME MARCHING HOME

A Mother's Story of the Price for Freedom

Rhonda Winfield

WHEN JOHNNY DOESN'T COME MARCHING HOME
A Mother's Story of the Price for Freedom

Caisson Press / June 2006
Book Jacket Design by Amber Dail

Library of Congress Control Number: 2006925801
ISBN: hardcover 1928724078

Manufactured in the United States of America

OTHER BOOKS FROM CAISSON PRESS

*Fallujah, With Honor, First Battalion, Eighth Marine's Role in
Operation Phantom Fury*

An Nasiriyah, The Fight for the Bridges

Tears of Ice, The Littlest Soldiers

Cradled In Glory, The Georgia Military Institute

Among the Best Men the South Could Boast, The Fall of Fort McAllister

Fields of Gray, The Battle of Griswoldville
All written by Gary Livingston

I Am My Brother's Keeper, Journal of a Gunny in Iraq
Written by Gunnery Sergeant Jason K. Doran, USMC (Ret)

LAST CALL

Howdy Ma, I know it's 4am
I just wanted a chance to hear your voice again
Thanks for all you've done
I was always proud to be your son.

I need you not to worry 'cause I'm almost home
Just one final mission then I'll be landin' back on
That sacred ground I've fought for
Another casualty of war.

They're gonna fly me into Dover with a flag on my chest
And I sure wish I could ride in on the bus with the rest
But it just can't be
Freedom isn't really free.

I was proud to serve though I hated to leave
Sometimes you've got to pay the price for what you believe
And in the late of the night when you're down on your knees
Thank God for those who've bought you all your liberties
I'm gonna miss you all
Just glad I had the chance to call.

Mamma, please be strong when they arrive in dress blues
You've feared all along that they would bring you the news
That I wouldn't be back
"Only two survived the attack"

I pray you won't get lost in a grief filled haze
You've still got my two baby brothers to raise
And they just can't see
You dyin' right along with me.

You'll tell them how I love them and they'll never walk alone
I'll always be beside them, not at the foot of a stone.
Tell them to talk to me
I gave my life to keep them free.

I was proud to serve though I hated to leave
Sometimes you've got to pay the price for what you believe.
And in the late of the night when you're down on your knees
Thank God for those who've bought you all your liberties
I'm gonna miss you all
Just glad I had the chance to call.

As the tears stream down my face and I have to let you go
I'll say, "I love you" and I'll pray that you'll know
It's always been that way
You made me the man I am today!

And I was proud to serve though I hated to leave
Sometimes you've got to pay the price for what you believe.
And in the late of the night when you're down on your knees
Thank God for those who've bought you all your liberties
I'm gonna miss you all
Just glad I had the chance to call.....

Howdy Ma, I know it's 4am.

WRITTEN BY RHONDA WINFIELD

FIRST LETTER
READ BY BRAD ARNOLD

A LETTER FROM A SOLDIER ABOUT TO PARTICIPATE IN
A LARGE AMERICAN OFFENSIVE JUST ONE MONTH
BEFORE THE END OF WORLD WAR I.

SEPTEMBER 11, 1918

*"THE [HARSH] CHARACTER OF THE COUNTRY MAKES
THE TASK WHICH WE FACE EXTREMELY DIFFICULT,
AND THE LOSSES ARE ALMOST CERTAIN TO BE
CONSIDERABLE. SUCCESS, HOWEVER, WILL MEAN SO
MUCH THAT ALMOST ANY PRICE WOULD BE CHEAP TO
PAY FOR IT. SHOULD I GO UNDER, THEREFORE, I
WANT YOU TO KNOW THAT I WENT WITHOUT ANY
TERROR OF DEATH, AND THAT MY CHIEF WORRY IS
THE GRIEF MY DEATH WILL BRING TO THOSE SO DEAR
TO ME. THERE HAS BEEN MUCH TO MAKE LIFE SWEET
AND GLORIOUS, BUT DEATH, WHILE DISTASTEFUL, IS
IN NO WAY TERRIBLE.*

*I FEEL WONDERFULLY STRONG TO DO MY SHARE
WELL, AND, FOR MY SAKE, YOU MUST TRY TO DROWN
YOUR SORROW IN THE PRIDE AND SATISFACTION, THE
KNOWLEDGE THAT I DIED WELL IN SO CLEAN A CAUSE,
AS OURS, SHOULD BRING YOU. REMEMBER HOW
PROUD I HAVE ALWAYS BEEN OF YOUR PLUCH, KEEP
MY BOYS' FUTURES IN MIND, AND DON'T PERMIT MY
DEATH TO BOW YOUR HEAD."*

*As researched and read by Brad Arnold at the funeral
service for LCPL Jason C. Redifer.*

Thank you for such a gift, Brad.

SECOND LETTER
READ BY BRAD ARNOLD

A LETTER FROM A RED CROSS NURSE AS SHE WRITES
A MOTHER ABOUT THE RECENT BURIAL OF HER SON,
JUST TWO DAYS AFTER THE END OF WORLD WAR I.

NOVEMBER 1918

*"A BIG HILL OVERSHADOWS THE PLACE AND THE SUN
WAS SETTING BEHIND IT JUST AS THE CHAPLAIN SAID
THE LAST PRAYER OVER YOUR BOY.*

*HE PRAYED THAT THE PEOPLE AT HOME MIGHT HAVE
GREAT STRENGTH NOW FOR THE BATTLE THAT IS
BEFORE THEM, AND WE DO ASK THAT FOR YOU NOW.*

*THE COUNTRY WILL ALWAYS HONOR YOUR BOY,
BECAUSE HE GAVE HIS LIFE FOR IT, AND IT WILL ALSO
LOVE AND HONOR YOU FOR THE GIFT OF YOUR BOY,
BUT BE ASSURED, THAT THE SACRIFICE IS NOT IN
VAIN, AND THE WORLD IS BETTER TODAY FOR IT."*

As researched and read by Brad Arnold at the funeral
service for LCPL Jason C. Redifer.

It is all truly not in vain and we are, indeed, better for it.
Thank you.

Praise for
When Johnny Doesn't Come Marching Home

Amid the daily headlines cataloging the latest US lives lost in Iraq, When Johnny Doesn't Come Marching Home is a vivid and heartfelt reminder of the effect of these deaths on mothers, families and communities across America. In laying bare her life and her grief Rhonda Winfield has written not just a tribute to her son Jason, but a book that ought to be read by anyone wanting to understand the human impact of war on those back home.

Mathew Davis, BBC Reporter

This story is about the triumph of the human spirit in the midst of personal tragedy. While I disagree with the reasons we went to war in Iraq, I am truly inspired by Rhonda Winfield's amazing journey to make sense out of a deep and heartrending loss, and move forward with courage and grace. Rhonda's brave son, Jason, gave his life in Iraq for what he believed in, and as she tells her (and his) powerful story, she takes the reader through a personal struggle of confusion, anger, and despair, indeed she confronts her worst fears inwardly and outwardly, and begins to emerge on a path to healing, restoration, and hope. For anyone who has lost a loved one, and wants to understand how they may be able to move beyond the bitterness and pain, Rhonda's story is a must read. I can see where Jason got his noble character from as the two of them, mother and son, merge together in this unforgettable story.

Nicholas Patler, author of *Jim Crow and the Wilson Administration: Protesting Federal Segregation in the Early Twentieth Century*, and contributor to *Peace Review: A Journal of Social Justice.*

...The book deals with the loss of one of our own and infuses our institution with a sense of humanity that is rooted in our history and nobility. It displays the naked truth of a family brought to its' knees by the sacrifice of a young Marine. It is written with a tender honesty that rips straight to the core of anyone who has a friend or family member serving in the military.

After reading this book, I am reminded of three things. First, families are forever changed after the loss of a loved one. Second, the Marine Corps takes care of their own. Third, America will never lose her freedoms as long as men and women like Jason C. Redifer rise to defend her. Whoever reads this book will come away with a higher respect and understanding of what it means to be a United States Marine.

2nd Lt Craig W. Thomas, USMC
Public Affairs, Headquarters and Support Battalion
Marine Corps Base Camp Lejeune

Acknowledgements

Thank you to my friends and family who supported me during the difficult process of putting my heart on paper. I appreciate everyone who volunteered to proofread, edit and critique, as well as those that helped make contacts and send out manuscripts. You labored in the hope that I would someday be able to share Jason's story with those that would otherwise not know it. Thank you to everyone who gave of themselves to make this dream a reality. I am especially grateful to Gary and Terry, of Caisson Press, for giving breath to my manuscript.

Thank you to those who did everything from offering your computers when mine crashed to those who held me when my heart broke. I love you all.

Thank you to our extended family, the United States Marine Corps. I will forever be a mother to the fine men of the 1 /2 Alpha Company. Your courage, bravery and devotion to one of your own have humbled me. I have learned that Marines LIVE Semper Fi and every one I have encountered on this journey has embraced me, uplifted me and reminded me that "once a Marine mom, always a Marine mom." HOORAH!

Lastly, a special thank you to Courtland and Carter who never seemed to grow tired of hearing, "Mommy just needs to finish one more paragraph..."

DEDICATION

This book is dedicated in admiration and loving memory to the late Father J. Kevin Fox. He was a scholar, a mentor, an inspiration and a true gentleman. He taught by example and was the epitome of excellence through discipline. He will be forever missed.

FOREWORD

On January 31, 2005 we both died. Jason died first, me a few hours later. He died on foreign soil as the result of a bomb exploding directly beneath the seat in which he rode in a Humvee. I died as the result of hearing the most devastating news a mother can hear. He left this world. I was damned to walk here without him. I, too, had injuries from the explosion. The hole that was blasted through my very center was raw and bleeding and sucking air. I tried to hold it closed, but there was too much damage. I covered it, learned to breathe around it and pretended for the comfort of others that it wasn't there. Yet every minute of every day the infection surrounding the hole worsened. For Jason, it was sudden and unexpected and over. For me, it was just beginning.

CHAPTER 1

THE PRAYER

"Our dearest Heavenly Father, we thank you for letting us come together today with our friends and family, who for us, are one and the same. We are so blessed to be able to surround Jason today, Lord, and remind him of our love and support for him. As he is about to embark on a noble journey, we pray, Father, that you will help him to always remember who he is, where he is from, what he stands for and that those who love him are at home waiting for his safe return. When there are times, Lord, that he is afraid, we pray that you will remind him that you always walk alongside him and if he is unable to make that walk, that you will carry him. Enfold him in your gracious arms and deliver him back unto our bosom safely, Lord.

We pray for your troops as they are fighting a battle for our freedom. Keep them strong and steadfast, surefooted on the path of righteousness. We pray, Our Heavenly Father, for our President and all those who advise him. May you grant them wisdom, bravery and perseverance. We also pray that while Jason is away that you will grant us patience, courage and a little extra faith. Help us to encourage and support one another while Jason is away. Please bring all our troops home safely, quickly and in the light of victory.
We ask all this in your name. Amen."

On June 12th 2004, I prayed that prayer in front of a yard full of guests at our farm in Stuarts Draft, Virginia. It was the day before Jason left. We gathered for a picnic in his honor. We wanted to give Jason a sendoff full of love and support. None of us knew what to do with the overwhelming fear we had been holding since the announcement of his deployment came, but like most families, we knew that food and fellowship were bound to help. We had to be strong for Jason. We all wanted one last opportunity to remind him of our love and

1

devotion. We all pretended that day was a launching of a big adventure. The truth was that war had come to our very home and no one had any idea what to do now that it was beyond our television set and in our very laps.

I had never publicly prayed before, with the exception of at mealtime with the family. Surprisingly, I wasn't even nervous. Somehow, I knew the words would come. Jason knew that I was more than proud of him. I needed him now to know that I was in awe of the man he had become in only nineteen years and that he was, long before ever going off to war, my hero. I told him so shortly after the prayer. These words flowed with ease. They were my words of goodbye. I believe that in my heart I knew even then what "goodbye" meant this time.

I think my husband, Scott, felt that I was being overly dramatic. I'm sure I embarrassed him on several levels that day but after fourteen years of marriage it was a feeling that he was not a stranger to. He cautioned me not to get myself into a panic. After all, military members participated in family picnics, went off on their assignments and came home to more family picnics. It was not a wake, for crying out loud. I have wondered many times since then if he really believed all that he said to me that day or if he was just not allowing himself to think the unthinkable. After all, we had never known anyone who had been killed in service. That was the sort of thing that happened in wars that we learned about from history books. This was 2004! The first Gulf War was short and I hoped that in the worse case scenario Jason would come home with some battle tales for his friends. Better yet for his friends, he would come home with some women of the world tales and be an even bigger hero!

Most of those gathered that day fell somewhere in between our two different states of being. They were festive but concerned. We were all proud to be sharing Jason with the Marines of Alpha Company, 1st Battalion, 2nd Marines, but we were all too aware that those very Marines were about to be engaged in a six month deployment to Iraq.

We all made index cards with encouraging words on them for him to take along with him. It was my hope that when he felt alone or frightened or homesick, that he could reach in his pocket and read each personal message in the writer's own hand, and find a bit of comfort from a place all his own. They all came back to me later with his personal affects from Iraq. He had done exactly that. I am certain that there was not one among us that day that could have envisioned the power those little cards held. It seemed almost a little childish to write them and I felt like the host at a baby shower announcing that a silly, pointless little game would be played, most likely involving diapers. Everyone was happy to indulge me and some took it very seriously. The fact that Jason had them with his personal belongings at the time of his death was a testament to the strength they brought him.

Justin and Jason's father was unable to attend the picnic. While Justin was close to his dad, Jason had not been, especially during the last several years. As with all divorces, children are the casualties. Ours was no exception. The fallout of our marital war left Jason and his father relatively alienated. While Jason's pride prevented him from having to make yet another attempt to reach out to his dad, he worried over whether or not he should try once again before he left. I encouraged him to do so. I convinced him that he did not want to find himself on the other side of the world, wishing he had another chance to make things right with his father. He took my advice and while he never really said what transpired between the two of them on the day he went to visit, I knew it was what he had been seeking. He could leave now with no regrets and no words left unspoken. He had made it a point to say goodbye to his father. I knew that even though his absence was felt on this day, it was not as though there was unfinished business between the two of them.

I invited my former in-laws to the picnic for Jason. I never considered not doing so. These people were Justin and Jason's family and rather than having Jason run all over the state trying to visit everyone to say farewell, it just made sense that we all gather in one place and do it together. Scott and I both felt that while a little awkward, it all seemed right.

The amount of food was shameless and we all ate until we could hold no more. I had a cake made with Jason's official Marine Corps photo on top. When I had gone to pick it up, the lady at the bakery recognized him from the photo. After all, his face now could serve fifty. She began to cry as she was ringing me up and finally had to excuse herself before the transaction was finished. When she returned to the register, she apologized and told me what a fine young man he was and how much he would be missed by her son who had known Jason for years, and all their friends. I was so moved by her emotional response that once I returned to the safety of my car, I opened my heart and cried full-throttle. I had needed to cry for days but was unprepared to have it drawn out by the sweet cake lady. I didn't share my trauma with anyone at the picnic as I divided his baked and frosted image into serving size pieces and we all rejoiced at how moist he was.

I watched both of my oldest sons interact that day in ways I had not seen since they were very small. They had always managed to tolerate one another but for the sake of outsiders, they never let it be forgotten that they were brothers. They had, however, suffered a distance in their relationship as Jason grew further away from his father. Justin's marriage to a beautiful and wonderful girl helped to begin to bridge this gap. Jason was so proud to have her for a sister-in-law and loved her deeply. I was able to see the three of them emerge into real adulthood together and I think they created a synergy that sustained each of them.

I watched as my two oldest sons embraced one another. I saw them let tears trickle down their cheeks. I was sure they had not seen one another cry since they were more than five years old. I heard them declare unabashedly their love for one another. The sound of it seemed such a contrast to their usual banter back and forth regarding Army vs. Marine Corps. Justin had enlisted into the Army first, and we joked all along that it was the single greatest factor into sending Jason straight into the Marine Corps. They had not said, "I love you" to one another in words since they were children. This time it wasn't because one had hurt the other and the words were being forced along with an apology. This hurt was greater than either had ever known and they both realized the importance of saying the words. I whispered to one of my life long friends who was watching with me, "I know he won't be coming home now." She didn't flinch or try to tell me that I was just being too worrisome, as so many did in the days following. She simply looked at me as the tears spilled down her cheeks and we shared an understanding that no one else was privy to at that time. She, too, saw what I knew.

The next morning as Jason packed, I sat in his room with the heaviest heart I had ever known. The finality of every move was weighing on me. He had made me have his dress blues uniform dry cleaned the day before so it would be ready, just in case. He thought it would be one less thing for me to have to tend to should the worst come to pass. Neither of us knew that he would be provided one at Dover when his body was flown home. I tried to tell myself that with so many things, if you are prepared, then you could hopefully spare yourself the dreaded thing that you are preparing against. I prayed this would be the case. I was quite proud that he had wanted it done. It was just another example of how he was always thinking of what would be best for me. He had taken the time to write, in his most child-like penmanship, a simple last will and testament. He knew he had few Earthly belongings, for one doesn't seem to accumulate much along those lines before age twenty. He valued what he had though as much as anything I have collected in all my years.

He wrote that "in the unlikely event of his death" that his horse, Lady, was to be given to his friend, Josh. He didn't care what Josh did with her. It was just enough to be able to let him know that he loved him enough to give him something he held so dear. He wanted his car, which he had only had for a few months, to go to his friend, James. This was if James wanted it and could afford to pay it off. I think in the end this proved too difficult a daily reminder for James, who by this time had purchased a vehicle of his own. The only other thing of value, Jason knew, would be the life insurance money that would follow. These funds were to be used to insure his younger brothers' education and the rest was to go to me to make the rest of our lives easier in whatever ways I saw fit. He trusted me to know just what to do with it. He left instructions for his funeral, including the songs he wanted to have played. He was precise about their order. He left the minor details for me, he said, but my guideline was to adhere to SIMPLICITY. He signed and dated the document at the bottom and showed me that it would await me, along with his other important military paperwork, in his desk drawer. Then, the subject was closed.

I thought the manner in which he began packing was almost funny, although I was entirely too distraught to manage a chuckle. He chatted about insignificant things, mainly to keep the heavy gravity of the situation from settling in. My sister-in-law, Avis, dropped by with a few things for him to take along. When I tried to speak to her, the flood of emotion began. She gave Jason some Matchbox cars that some of her co-workers had sent. They thought he could possibly hand them out to some Iraqi children. We later learned that Jason had approached a few children beside the road while on a patrol and did just that. The children, in their excitement, pointed ahead, telling Jason where some explosive devices had been placed that his unit was unexpectedly about to stumble upon. How cheap the price for American lives, only $3.00 worth of die cast toys for twenty U.S. Marines. Jason later said that the most frightening thing of all that day was not how close they came to death, but how those children knew what was ahead for the Americans and were patiently waiting beside the road to watch.

He rolled and packed and stuffed, not only all of his basic necessities, but anything else that said HOME to him. I remembered that in boot camp, against regulations, he had taped pieces of photos inside his Kevlar helmet to bring him strength when he needed it most. His photo collage content was simple: his current girlfriend, his brothers, his mother and his horse. All the things that he thought he needed to protect back home, in one shape or another, were taped inside.

The last items he packed that day were his cowboy boots. I actually managed a laugh. How perfectly Jason.

I reminded him that they were still not standard military issue, as far as I knew, and that he probably would not be allowed to wear them with his desert BDU's (Battle Dress Uniform). He grinned his mischievous grin and told me that he had never been without them. He needed that piece of himself with him. Those boots symbolized Jason the man, not Jason the Marine. He folded them up as much as possible, rolling the tops down around the bottoms, thereby almost insuring that they could never be worn again. They were pretty worn out, as it was. He placed them so gently and carefully in his pack. They too, came home in his box of personal affects. His brother, Justin, would eventually lift them out of the box as gingerly as Jason had placed them in. He would carefully unroll them, hold them tightly to his chest and then somehow manage to slide them onto his feet. I have no idea how a person walks in someone else's cowboy boots, even under the best of circumstance, but Justin wears these, with great pride and devotion to his brother, to this day. Love is all that is still holding them together.

Jason squashed everything down into his bag, managed to get it zipped and then gave me the look that told me the time had come. It was absolutely useless to even try to hold it back. My emotions came boiling up from within me like lava being tossed from a newly awakened volcano. I heard myself spew forth an almost primal cry that originated from somewhere so deep from within my being that it was foreign to me. I knew the significance of this moment, yet I was powerless to change the inevitable. This was my forever. I could not even look at him as he stood there in that doorway so brave and certain. I tried to reach for him but my body faltered me and instead backed further away. He told me that it was now or never and if I couldn't do it, he'd just have to go without it. I ran to the bathroom, vomited, rinsed my mouth, washed my face and returned with all of the courage I could muster. We embraced with all the love we had and said our "I love you's." Unable to even stand on my own, Scott held me by the waist as we watched him walk off our porch. As I was thinking about how much he loved sitting on this very porch on summer nights, listening to the crickets and talking, he turned around one last time.

"I love ya, Ma!" he shouted and then flashed me his million watt smile. I never saw him again.

The Marines Prayer

Almighty Father, whose command is over all and whose love never fails, make me aware of Thy presence and obedient to Thy will. Keep me true to my best self, guarding me against dishonesty in purpose in deed and helping me to live so that I can face my fellow Marines, my loved ones and Thee without shame or fear. Protect my family.

Give me the will to do the work of a Marine and to accept my share of responsibilities with vigor and enthusiasm. Grant me the courage to be proficient in my daily performance. Keep me loyal and faithful to my superiors and to the duties my country and the Marine Corps have entrusted to me. Make me Considerate of those committed to my leadership. Help me to wear my uniform with dignity, and let it remind me daily of the traditions, which I must uphold.

If I am inclined to doubt, steady my faith; if I am tempted, make me strong to resist; if I should miss the mark, give me courage to try again. Guide me with the light of truth and grant me wisdom by which I may understand the answer to my prayer. Amen.

CHAPTER 2

THE NEWS

We had been too afraid to actually believe in it. We had learned the hard way that the military has its own time line and way of doing things to which civilians were not privy. Too many countless hours had been spent waiting in a hot car, in some parking lot, on some base, not knowing if we were in the right place to even have a chance to see Jason, much less pick him up for home. So, when Jason had been telling us that he was in the final countdown to coming home from Iraq, we were scared to let ourselves fully believe. As the time got closer, I began to make "Welcome Home" signs in preparation for our visit to Camp LeJeune to welcome home our Marines. Scott warned me not to get too prepared. I decided these little gestures would be all right. Even if the homecoming would be postponed, we could still use these things at a later date. Scott, who had been forced to watch me grieve myself into an unhealthy mental and physical disaster since Jason was deployed, very much feared my stability if, in fact, the homecoming was postponed. We had been hearing over and over of many tours being extended and I was praying nightly that Jason's would not be one of them.

Finally, on the morning of January 31, 2005, I received a phone call at 4:00am. Jason was calling to say that he was coming home. He only had a minute to talk, but his unit was heading out on their final patrol of the mission. Just one more time going door to door, sweeping the roads and making an appearance to remind the insurgents of their presence and then it was back to camp to begin packing for the good ol' USA! We had spoken only days before of the success of the first ever free Iraq elections. Jason felt there was a huge sense of relief in that there were far fewer problems than anticipated. There was also a far greater turnout. He spoke of what it was like to see grown men crying in the streets because they had witnessed a glimpse of democracy. I have thought so many times since then what it must have been like for those people to leave their homes that morning, not knowing if they would live to return. Yet, the concept of freedom was so important to them that they had gambled their very lives for a chance to vote. They weren't sure it would even matter when the day was through. They simply knew that if they did not take the chance, they would never have freedom and they felt that the taste of a free life was worth the risk. I will never forget the pictures I saw in the news of an Iraqi woman standing beside her husband, both proudly showing their ink-stained fingers. I thought of the struggle in this country for women to gain suffrage and though I had always felt pride as a woman voter in this country, I feel an even greater sense of responsibility in actually doing so now. I wondered how some Americans can feel so apathetic to their right to select their government and voice their opinions that they would skip going to the polls because it was raining, or perhaps they didn't want to wait in line. Do we know anyone around us who would go if they thought they might have to die to do it? Jason, and thousands of other young men and women like him, helped to make that process possible for people who probably never dreamt it could be. To say I was proud would be an understatement. So much about Jason had left me at a total loss for words.

I could tell by his voice in our previous conversation that he was tired and weary. Jason had been transformed during his six months there and every phone call made it more obvious. He tried to be himself and say all the "old Jason" kind of things but there was a haunt in his voice. He had emailed a photo home of himself and in his eyes there was a cold vacancy. They were not the soft, brown teddy bear eyes that he left with. They were dark, black windows into a soul that had been forever tattooed by evil. I made no pretenses. I knew that Jason was not coming home to us the same person who had left. I also knew that however Jason came home, we would be sure to give him everything he needed, most of which was the love that we all had for him. Jason and I had discussed it briefly and he knew that I was aware that he didn't even know what to expect from himself once he had the luxury of taking the time to look inwardly. He had told all of his friends to hold off on the celebration parties. He already knew that he was only going to try to see them, a few at a time, and was only going to do so from home for a while.

Jason was so proud of the car he had just purchased before leaving. It was a four door family sedan. He decided that if he was going to be in debt for so much money, he would just go ahead and get a car that would last him for a while. He wanted to make sure he bought one with plenty of room for the children he hoped to have one day. Jason told me in one of our last conversations that he wouldn't be able to drive himself home from Camp LeJeune, so if we were bringing the car for him, someone else would have to drive it back. He didn't know what to expect but he knew he wanted things to be as quiet as possible and he didn't want the responsibility of driving a vehicle. He had always loved to drive and had done so since he was about six years old. Living on a farm he had ample opportunity to be driving something all the time. He drove for his Staff Sergeant and his Lieutenant as part of his job and was proud to do so. It surprised me to hear him say that he would not know how to drive on civilian roads now.

Jason said he just wanted to get off that bus and get "his boys" in his arms. He was talking, of course, about Courtland and Carter, my two youngest sons. I think the hardest part of being away for him was seeing the photos of how quickly they were growing and he was desperately missing them. They truly were his boys and he could not have loved them more if they were his own children. He promised me that I would be next in line and then we were headed to eat. I asked where he wanted to go. He said that a few weeks before, someone in his unit had traveled to a larger base in Iraq that actually had a Burger King. His buddy brought back a Whopper to him, although the Whopper was four days old by the time Jason received it and had not been refrigerated. Factor that in with the desert heat. Jason said it was the best bite of food he had ever eaten. He shared it with his squad. He assured me that a little food poisoning was the least of their concerns. So, at that point, he decided that when he hit U.S. soil, it would be a trip to Burger King for him. He asked if his buddy, Lance

Corporal Harry Swain, could go with us. Harry had been the buddy that was sworn to call me if anything happened to Jason. Of course, Harry would go with us.

That night, I made a sign that said, "WELCOME HOME REDIFER, SWAIN AND DONKEY!"

Jason had been such a fan of the animated film, *Shrek*. While the children and I were Christmas shopping, we came across a stuffed "Donkey" character from the movie and I knew we had to send it to Jason. When sending him things we knew he would enjoy them with his friends and then most likely have to discard them. We didn't care. If it brought him a few minutes of laughter or made his day seem a little less dark, then it didn't matter. Well, apparently, Donkey was a hit with the whole platoon. Jason would walk around reciting all of Donkey's dialogue from the movie. If you squeezed the donkey's sides you would hear Eddie Murphy's voice spouting tidbits from the movie. Jason prided himself in his ability to do the same and either entertained or annoyed his buddies with it constantly. They even took turns carrying Donkey on patrols with them. How could I not include him in the homecoming? I had no idea the day I painted those names on that sign that Donkey would be the only one that would return.

After I learned of the final patrol that morning, (early afternoon Iraq time) I was elated! Jason, however, sounded more distant than ever. He was the most positive person I have ever known in my life but his last two calls were a far cry from the son I knew. He was exhausted, remote and calculated in what he said. We always joked around, even with the serious stuff. I played with him as usual and said, "You just make sure you get through this one and get home! You know that it would kill me if you didn't and then who would raise your brothers?" Normally, his response was that he would keep that in mind and would just have to make sure he got it done. I expected the same response that morning, but he surprised me by pausing and then saying simply, "I know, Ma." Our conversation was brief, as he was not supposed to even be on the phone and he ended as he always did. "Tell Scott I said Howdy, give my boys a hug and a kiss for me and remember, I love you, Ma." I responded in like and we hung up the phone. I was excited yet felt something was very strange. I never spoke to my son again.

I shared all the news with Scott and for the first time he allowed himself to believe that Jason was coming home as scheduled. We began to prepare. I was crazed with excitement and my mind reeled with all my plans for getting ready. I was a rural mail carrier and other post offices were standing by for the final word to switch carriers around so that someone would be available to cover my route for me to go. Postal employees all around were volunteering to do extra duties so that I could leave at a moment's notice. Everyone in our postal community had been following Jason's military journey from the day of his high school graduation until now and were all anxious to have him visit in his dress blues when he came home. He had already planned to take a day to spend with me just going around to personally thank everyone who had sent him cards, letters, emails, packages and those that just helped to support his mom. Jason wrote to everyone asking them to check on and to take care of his mother.

Justin, Jason and I literally grew up together and we had an incredibly close bond that transcended the normal parent-child. We were the guardians for one another. We had something that was too powerful to explain or put into words but that connected the three of us in an extraordinary way. Because Jason was the baby, he was closer to me. Justin was his own man, having left home at seventeen and that left Jason, in his mind, to fill in the gap. He did so with devotion and adoration and we were of one heart. We didn't always agree, but he always knew that I loved him and believed that I only wanted the best that life could offer him. He was never embarrassed to kiss me or tell me how much he loved me, even in public. If you knew Jason, you knew he loved his family. He had his priorities and God, his family and his country topped the list.

As I encountered friends in the postal realm that day, I took the time to tell everyone of my fabulous, long-awaited news. It was probably the most relaxed day I had experienced since he left for Iraq. Everyone rejoiced with me as we began the countdown for the nine days that were left standing between me and my son. I drove home that evening with the sun at my back. It was a beautiful day for January. I couldn't wait to get inside to help Courtland and Carter start making their signs. They were so excited to know that Jason was on his way home to them. The many long months of sending photos and pictures they had drawn, not to mention waiting anxiously every day by the mailbox were soon to end. I remember the smile on my face that I had worn all day. As I turned into my driveway, I saw the white van parked in my space. My heart sank and I said a quick prayer under my breath asking that the van not be bearing government tags. Every next of kin knows that if your loved one is injured, you will be notified by phone. If they are dead, you will receive the information in person. The van had government tags. My mind quickly kicked into survival mode and I began to flash through all the possible reasons that a government vehicle could be here. Since Scott was a dairy farmer, I quickly assessed that the vehicle would belong to someone in a government agency that dealt with milk regulation, perhaps. I grabbed my cell phone and started to dial Scott's cell number, my heart pounding out of my chest. I have heard that in a crisis your whole life can literally flash before your eyes. I had an entire phone conversation flash before mine. In my mind's eye, Scott had answered the phone, I had asked about the white van and he had explained it away as something routine regarding the dairy and I had laughed, telling him of my near panic attack. In reality, I dialed only a few digits when I was stopped by something I saw from the corner of my eye. Coming around the house was Scott, flanked by two Marines in dress blues. A uniform that made young Marines the sharpest dressed of all the military branches; that uniform they were all so proud to wear; that uniform that told the world what they stood for-earned, never given. In that moment, that uniform came into my field of vision now cloaked upon the angel of death. I remember saying, "Oh my, God," I do not remember actually getting out of the Jeep. I looked at Scott as the three of them were moving toward me in slow motion and I yelled out his name. Why was he not realizing what horror I was thinking and immediately tell me what a mistake I was making? Why was he not immediately announcing why these men were here? Scott opened his mouth after what seemed like an eternity, but he could only tell me that I needed to come into the yard and talk with these gentlemen. He told me that they would not tell him why they were here. That was when the cannonball fired. I don't know what direction it came from, but it hit me squarely in my middle, somewhere just below my breasts and above my hips. It was an enormous hole and as I struggled to grab some breath, I spoke out in a low guttural sound that was somewhere between a question and a command. The sound was so foreign to me and I just assumed that was because of the hole in my being. I said, "Don't you dare be here to tell me that something has happened to my son." The Marine in closest proximity to my husband was now stopped in his place and simply lowered his head in a most reverent manner and crossed his white-gloved hands in front of himself. I remember thrusting myself forward at this moment, unable to ignore the wheezing hole in myself any longer. All of my life was springing forward out of me, my wound raw and gaping and sucking wind. I throbbed with pain; I felt myself spin with dizziness. The nausea swept over me and blackness danced around inside my head. I could hear myself, or someone who sounded like me, saying over and over again, "NO! NO! NO! NO!" I swayed to the tempo of it and gasped between words until I was almost on the ground. I heard Scott buzzing closer to my ears and was finally able to focus on his face. I don't know what he was saying but I understood that he needed me to come into the house. Something snapped at that very moment and I stood up and stepped outside of myself. I left that broken, bleeding, dying girl in that death mire in the driveway and pulled myself up to my husband, whom I let lead me inside. I could feel the uniforms following us.

I told the new me that I had to focus. Crisp, clear, certain. I was about to be given information that I would never again have the chance to hear. I was going to be given all that I was getting of Jason and I had to prepare. I think that in the heart of every mother who saw her child leave for war, there is the place that has played out the worst scenario over and over. It is a movie you have created in your mind. The details are vivid and complete.

You know how it will all play out. It is indeed the worst and perhaps it is something that we do to prepare ourselves in the event that it becomes our reality. I know that day, that the movie in my mind hit auto play and what was so familiar to me in only the dark recess of my thoughts was now in full screen Technicolor for the whole world to see. I was afraid I would not be able to drink in every syllable of what Captain S.D. Pharathikoune, USMC, had come to tell me. I knew that I would play those details over and over again in my mind for the rest of time and I needed the recall to be complete. All that I would ever know about my son now was going to come from this stranger. Hard as I tried and as thorough as I know he was, I cannot tell you much of what he said. The cinema flashes kept interrupting. I knew exactly what Jason's face looked like in that nanosecond before death. I had seen it in my nightmares. I had read many times in my life that the last words a soldier cries out in death are for his mother. I heard him scream. I saw his face and I didn't even know what had happened yet. Iskandariyah! Improvised explosive device! Mortally wounded! Trauma! More information forthcoming! Dead!

They were reading me the time of death and I interrupted them. No way! They were in my living room telling me that my son was killed, on his last f***ing patrol, just nine days before he was to be back in this same living room and only two f***ing hours after talking to me on the phone? I was only able to verbalize to them that I had just spoken to him right before that. Captain P. (as he instructed us, at some point, to call him) seemed to understand the rest. I will never be able to tell anyone what those Marines conveyed to me that day. Yes, the worst news of my life came with them but it came to me in the package of brother Marines who were already grieving a loss I had yet to be informed of. The respect and honor for my son and my family that they were able to portray in every step of this horrific path was just another sordid piece of this kaleidoscope of feelings and emotions. The best, bringing the worst. The official part was over relatively quickly and I looked at them as if expecting something more and they looked at me likewise. Eventually, when neither side came forth, Captain P. announced that they would be going and would return to us the following morning. "We will be taking our leave now," he said. I had never heard that particular expression before. I have heard it in my mind many times since.

When they went out of the door, I just looked at Scott. I wanted to just say, "I TOLD YOU SO." I had grieved myself sick since the day Jason had left. A part of me knowing he wasn't coming home to me, and a part of me not wanting to give in to that. Scott would always say, "statistically speaking, he is in far greater danger of having something happen to him here out driving at night with his teenage friends." It would make me insane! Statistically speaking, hell! I looked up at him from the lowest point in my life and wanted to say the words but wouldn't allow myself. I could see all over his face that it was exactly those words that were already ringing in his ears and even though I tried to spare him by not blubbering out what I thought, my face had already betrayed me. We began to talk about it briefly but I changed gears again and told him that we would have to put whatever we were feeling on hold. There was work to be done. After all, I knew what to do at this point. I had practiced this part of it over and over in my mind. I had to move on, the next scene had already begun.

Still trying to hold my attention, Scott was attempting to tell me what had transpired before my arrival home. He was running the previews for me but I didn't need the theatrical trailer now. I was already closing Act I of the feature presentation. He was telling me that he and the children had gone next door to his parents so that he could help move a piece of furniture. The children were playing in my in-law's basement and never heard the Marines at the door. They apparently tried our house first and when no one answered, moved across the lawn. They had asked for me and Scott told them that I should be arriving home at any minute. He knew what dress blues meant as well as I did but they couldn't give him the official word since I was the next of kin.

I don't know how much time elapsed until our minister, Rev. B. Failes, arrived or how he had even gotten the word. In my memory it seems as though he almost passed the Marines on their way out. We decided to get the children home and sit them down to tell them the news before people started coming. We didn't want them to accidentally hear it from someone other than us. I had no idea what to say to them. This was not in the script. With Rev. B. beside me, I opened my mouth, not knowing at all what to say and, as I had that day at the picnic, I began to speak without any idea of what was coming out. I cannot begin to tell you today what I said or even how I said it. I just know that when it was over I asked Rev. B if that was O.K. He didn't seem to indicate that I had screwed it up terribly. Of course, even if I had, I'm sure he wouldn't have said so at that point. Besides, it wasn't as if it could be undone now anyway. The bell had already been rung. There were no retakes here. I kept feeling at the time, and have continued to feel ever since, that there should be something more that I could give Courtland and Carter. There should be something reasonable and matter of fact and concrete and comforting and there was not.

Carter, at age six, was shocked but seemed to regroup quickly and I wasn't sure just how much he comprehended. How much did I even comprehend? Courtland, at eight, was leveled and cried so hard that I thought, he too, might break.

I had to call Justin and break the news to him over the phone since he and his wife, Missy, were living in Lewisburg, West Virginia. I am not sure at what point I did that. The first person I spoke with was Justin and Jason's dad. He lived only about twenty minutes from me and had been visited by dress blues as well. We just hung on the phone in silence and disbelief and agony. How ironic. It was probably the first thing we had truly shared since the birth of our children. The Alpha and the Omega.

Justin had served a one-year deployment in Fort Stewart, Georgia with the 304th Military Police Company Detachment of the U.S. Army Reserve Unit of Lewisburg, West Virginia. His unit had been called to Georgia under Operation Noble Eagle to cover for the 3rd Infantry Division while they were serving in Afghanistan and Iraq during Operation Enduring Freedom. After his return from

Georgia, he relocated to be near his U.S. Army Reserve Center and now lived and worked in Lewisburg.

I tried to call Justin several times and was unable to reach him. I called his landlord, who was also his employer, and asked if he could find him. I was obviously rather upset and he inquired. I explained and asked if he could find Justin and stay with him while he called home. I didn't want him to be alone to hear this so coldly over the phone. It was a terrible thing to ask, I know, and I hate now that I did. How unfair! The phone rang about ten minutes later and it was Justin. He was very shaken and said only, "what happened?" As I began to give him the details, he interrupted and asked, "how bad is it?" I was taken aback in the sudden realization that he didn't know the full scope of the situation. I had to tell him flatly and coldly that his brother was dead. Just like that. No buffer, no comforting words, no human touch. Just the poison arrow of death shot through a phone line. He was on his way and would arrive in just under two hours. I was worried for his safety and that of Missy, his wife, as they drove such a distance with the shock of the news so fresh and heavy. In my twisted warp of time, he was home in minutes.

In many ways, Justin and I have not let go of one another since we fell together as he made his way into the house that day. He became the lone lifeline for his father in the months to come.

I went into Jason's room and picked up a silly stuffed monkey we had sent to him for his birthday. We had hoped it would make him smile because we had always teased him about looking like a monkey himself as a baby. He mailed it back home with a few things that he wanted to be certain would arrive safely in the U.S. I picked up "Mr. Monkey," as we would refer to him in the months to come, and doused him with my tears. I did not let him go for months and he can still be found periodically in my purse, just out of sight.

Scott and I went to pick up my mother who lives alone. We gave her the news and brought her back to our house. Mechanically, I went through my address book and called all of the people that I could think of that should be notified immediately. The wheels were in motion. The night became its own entity.

I have no recollection of time or space, just isolated events and people. Finally, the point came where I felt the floor going out from under me and knew I had to go lie down. Scott and I went upstairs to bed. There would be no sleeping. I rested for a little while and we talked until there seemed to be no more words, just pain. I went into the bathroom and drew a hot bath. When the tub could hold no more water, I slipped into the steamy bath and just imagined myself disappearing completely into it. I tilted my head back and envisioned what it would feel like to just slide beneath the surface and let it all completely wash over me. I would stay that way. I would take it all into my lungs and hold it there until there was nothing but the blackness. I wanted so desperately to give into it. I could feel the hot water begin to pour across my face and quickly my lungs began to burn. Specs of light danced behind my eyes. I tried to settle my head tightly on the bottom of the tub to wait for my eternity to come. Suddenly, I felt the arms reach under me and sit me upright. They were gentle, yet firm, and they understood. When I wiped the tears and bath water from my eyes I was not surprised to find no one. The arms that lifted me back to the surface were no longer of this life.

I climbed out of the tub, barely dried myself off and went to Scott in the bed. I didn't even bother to put on a nightgown. I just asked him to hold me as tightly as he could. We lay there together for hours, just softly talking while our tears mingled together down our cheeks. I have used the phrase "a broken heart" all my life, but it was that night that I truly knew what it really meant. I could physically feel the pain in my heart where it had shattered. I felt if Scott let me go that it would fly apart in a million directions, so he held me together and whispered to me until somewhere in the darkness the grace of the nighttime found me and gave me some peace. I didn't sleep long but while I did, I rested with the most comfort that I had since Jason had left. For the first time in six months, I didn't have to worry about my son. He was safe now. He was truly home.

CHAPTER 3

ARLINGTON DECISION

When the two Marines returned the morning of February 1, 2005, it was to provide us with more information and perhaps reiterate some of the information given the evening before. I really couldn't say with any certainty all that was told to me on that visit. Then, just several hours after bringing the news that would stop my life, they were back again for "Phase II", as I would later refer to it. During the endless hours of the night, I longed for their return. Anything associated with their presence would be something a step closer to Jason. In the light of morning, as I watched them come through my front door, my heart stopped again. With them, they brought death. No matter how empathetic and kind, professional and yet personal, they carried before them the finality of my child. They were not wearing their dress blues that day and this took me by surprise. It stung me. I felt as though we had passed through something that I was not yet ready to leave. The formality of bearing the news required the respect of the sharpest demeanor they had to offer and now he was just my dead kid to be dealt with. Now there was just the business of getting it all taken care of. Of course, never once did anyone behave in that manner, in fact, just the opposite is true. Every Marine that I have encountered since that day has embraced me in their hearts, as well as their arms and has felt my pain and loss in a way no other mortal could understand. I asked Captain P. at one point what he screwed up to get punished with such a lousy job. His eyes filled with tears and he told me with the most sincerity I had ever heard, that this was the highest honor a Marine could perform. I believed then, as I believe now, that he meant that with his whole heart.

The two Marines were dressed in BDU's, which wasn't exactly jeans and a T-shirt, but certainly a big step down from the previous evening. I forced myself on through the portal to "Phase II" even though I was extremely reluctant to do so. It was all going so fast. I was being sucked into a vacuum at the speed of light. I was trying to comprehend all that was being told to me, trying to just absorb the fact that my baby had been killed and trying to make all of the decisions that were being thrown at me. I had so many tasks to accomplish as well as trying to stay one step ahead of some things to make sure arrangements were made as Jason had wanted. The tidal wave of visitors had begun even before all of the family had assembled the previous evening and was only picking up momentum. The media had arrived before the "we're sorry to inform you" words had even dissipated into the air and the story was appearing on every television station, radio station and newspaper that we had ever heard of- and some, in fact, that we had not. I was anxious to speak with anyone that would listen to my voice. Many have questioned that and my ability to tell the story as I did. It was never an option to me. This was Jason's story. This was Jason's short life. I wanted the entire world to know what was lost the day he left us. I wanted every eye to shed a tear, every heart to hurt and every clock to stop for just a second. He had a lifetime of promise and opportunity ahead of him and he willingly gave it for his country. Every citizen needed to know about the young man who had just helped purchase their freedom with his life. I knew Jason was not the only casualty of this war. He was, however, my casualty. If they had a medium in which to take my pain and Jason's pride to the people, then I couldn't talk enough.

I sat on the sofa facing these imposing Marines. I found that I was very nervous in their presence. Perhaps it was a fear of what they may have yet to unveil. Perhaps I was uncomfortable in my own skin, not knowing the appropriate way to respond or react to things of such a foreign nature. I was concerned that I wasn't asking the right questions or providing the right answers. They were very tolerant and always helpful, yet there was a mighty canyon of distance between those that had lost and those that were trying to help the lost.

I have no idea what information was being given to me when I heard the words that told me Jason was eligible for burial at Arlington National Cemetery. Of all the plans he had written out prior to his deployment, he had never mentioned burial. I had never thought of it either. I was immediately relieved to think he would be resting in a place of such regard. My mind raced back to all of the visits I had made there growing up and of the times the children had been there on fieldtrips. I thought of John F. Kennedy and how Jason had quoted him in his senior page of the school yearbook.

Each of the seniors was given their own page in the Stuart Hall School yearbook to fill as they wished. Most chose family photos and fun memories. Jason's was unique. It has haunted us all. It is just further proof to me that he always knew that God had some special purpose for his life and that it wasn't going to be one of great length. He knew more than anyone I have ever known, that the quality of life here on Earth is far more important than the amount of time. He tried to fill everyday with as much joy as he could and encouraged others to do the same. His photos included various snapshots of fun he had on the farm, riding horses, herding cattle, playing a round of golf-in the snow-on horseback (dismounting to hit the ball) and a silhouette of him literally riding off into the sunset. He included a snapshot of his baby brother asleep under our English Bulldog, a few shots of fun with friends and most eerily a photograph of the New York skyline that he had taken while we were on a trip several years before. He took that same photograph with him to Iraq to look at the Twin Towers every day and remember why he was there. He quoted, "I'm here for a good time, not a long time." This annoyed me greatly at the time and I suggested that this would perpetuate the notion that he was a total redneck. Later, it proved to be haunting. His page contained several quotes that he truly lived by and they have become so significant to all who knew him since he died. *"Cowards die many times before their death; the valiant never taste of death but once."* William Shakespeare. He wasn't afraid to be valiant. He wouldn't tolerate cowardice. He also quoted, *"It is not what you take with you when you leave this world, but what you leave behind you when you go."* He took nothing. He left a legacy. He quoted Mark Twain with, *"Let us endeavor so to live that when we come to die even the undertaker will be sorry."* I believe he was. Franklin D. Roosevelt's, *"We have nothing to fear but fear itself"* was beside, *"The only limits life has are those you set for yourself."* He reminded us in the words of country music artist, Clay Walker, to *"Live, laugh, love"* and at the bottom of his page was *"God bless the USA"* and *"USMC-Semper Fi!"* The last quote was positioned directly under the Twin Tower photo. It was of JFK's *"Ask not what your country can do for you; ask what you can do for your country."* He would now rest with the man he so admired for speaking those words to a nation they were both devoted to.

There was some concern in my family that Jason would be so far from home. My mother, especially, knew that she would not have the freedom to visit his grave as often as she would like since she would have to rely on someone to take her to Arlington. While I honored these feelings, I couldn't help but feel as though he needed to be laid to rest in a place of honor and history among like souls and heroes. I wanted to be able to visit his grave in celebration and pride for who and what my son was and to honor the legacy he left, not just go mourn a sunken piece of ground. For me, it was about the difference between simply visiting death and loss compared to visiting a memorial of a life that embraced courage, honor, dedication and heroism. He would not be just among some dead there. He would be part of our nation's faithful. I wanted Courtland and Carter to look at all the famous names of people who upheld and shaped this country and to see their brother's name among them. I wanted Jason to be in a place of ceremony and reverence dedicated to those that answered the calling of a grateful country. There was no decision to be made here. Jason belonged in Arlington.

Like others buried there before him, Jason lived a life of valor. He was one squared away Marine. He was a mental, physical package. He was not only capable; he was capable under the pressures of combat. Since his death, our family has heard many incredible stories about the Marine that Jason was, as well as the man that he became. He liked to laugh and he loved to make others laugh. He never wanted anyone to forget the importance of play and often times this was not in keeping with the order of the day in Marine life. He had a penchant for being mischievous but was always willing to take the heat when the hammer fell. Jason was far from perfect, was certainly not infallible, and found more than his share of trouble. He was, however, all heart. He was honest and loyal. He was the epitome of friend. He tried to make every moment of his life a celebration and a party but when he had a job to do, he knew how to work and to accomplish his goals. Jason was dedicated and courageous. He was bold and he was tender. He had a sense of right and wrong and didn't care much for "gray areas." He was a cowboy. He was a hero. Jason would have simply told you that he was nothing special. That was just one more thing that made him exactly that.

Jason and Justin were four and five years old, respectively, when I remarried. Scott was a farmer and so the children and I went to live on his family's farm about thirty miles from where we had called home and the boys quickly came to love it. I have often said that we all grew up there. They had many responsibilities for their young ages and had seen way too much of the real world. Farm life is never easy but they were grateful for the life we had found there and flourished in their new environment. They loved working with the animals and never took for granted the fragile balance of nature and the miracle of life itself. They had vivid imaginations and seemingly endless acres of playground to play out anything they could dream up.

Justin was wise beyond his tender years. He deemed himself the "brains" of the two. Jason thought Justin was ten feet tall and bulletproof. He ate when Justin ate, stopped when Justin stopped. He looked to him when he needed to form an opinion and ran to him when he needed validation. As they grew, Jason found some autonomy and decided that maybe he should be "top dog." Regime change is never easy or smooth and the brothers polarized and waged battle frequently as hormones surfaced and manhood loomed in the distance. Despite his will and vigor, Jason would be so frustrated as his smaller stature kept him his brother's underling.

One day the boys had disappeared in the barn and didn't come when they were called for dinner. We finally heard them answer that they were on the way but still didn't show up for quite some time. When they did emerge, the door flew open and in blew two ragged, sweating, angry young men that were red in the face and filthy. They were obviously furious with one another and I thought we were lucky that they didn't fall onto the floor in a brawl right there. I couldn't get either one of them to come clean regarding what had just transpired, although I tried everything I could think of to threaten them. I saw that beneath that fuming face, Jason had tears welled up in his eyes. I decided to let it go before he ended up spilling them down his face, an embarrassment that he probably didn't need at that moment. Justin would have eaten his own head before he would have dropped a single tear in front of someone and Jason could well up at the drop of a hat if he thought you were truly angry with him. Over time, they both learned to find some middle ground.

It was much later on that the boys told me, separately, of the barn incident. They had apparently decided to settle one of their many petty arguments by beating one another until there was a clear winner. This method had always served Justin well since he was the bigger brother. Jason was determined that one day, though, he would catch up in stature and the tables would be forever turned. He decided that this would be the day. According to both, Jason never actually saw victory, but both boys realized that day, that he had in fact, finally grown enough to level the playing field a lot more in his favor. Justin still walked away the obvious victor but decided that in order to keep claim to his title, the fighting should probably end there. Jason did well enough to know that he had, indeed, succeeded in progressing to the ranks of a serious competitor with his brother. This was his victory. That day changed the dynamic between them. They found a new relationship within their brotherhood. They found respect for one another.

Justin still set the tone for the two, even though he never realized it and Jason never admitted it. He was the example. Sometimes it was the example of what to beat; sometimes it was the example of what not to do. Either way, he paved the path. I have often wondered if Jason decided to be a Marine because Justin joined the Army.

It certainly did provide interesting dinner conversation at family gatherings!

The boys both worked jobs to pay for their private education. Justin was attending a military school in preparation for a life in the service. He was always regimented and we saw this as a perfect fit for him. Jason, however.... We would never have thought that our little wisecracker who couldn't stop giggling would ever consider the military. We knew how deeply patriotic both boys were but Jason had a personality that would not have lead one to envision him thriving in a deeply disciplined environment. Again, I believe Justin set the tone. For high school, though, Jason decided that if he was paying his own tuition, he was going to go a different route altogether. Jason became the first male admitted to a previously all girls high school in Staunton, Virginia. Stuart Hall had been an Episcopal private boarding school for girls for almost 150 years and was deeply steeped in tradition. Financial concerns as well as several other factors led the school to consider the admission of boys as day students. I couldn't believe it when I realized that Jason was going to be the first. Dear God! Did they get the cock for the hen house right off the bat? Several of the teachers there remember seeing Jason on the day that he went for an orientation visit and just thought that he almost carried a neon sign that said "TROUBLE" above his Donnie Osmond smile and ten gallon hat. I'm quite sure that those sacred halls that had housed debutantes for generations were quite unaccustomed to the scuffling of cowboy boots.

Jason never missed a chance to remind Justin, who was being educated with an all-male class, that he had perhaps chosen the best "educational" path. Our entire family not only enjoyed Jason's years at Stuart Hall, but also came to love the school and all those associated with it as our family. Our "Stu" friends have suffered and grieved alongside us and they feel as though they have lost a son as well.

Father J. Kevin Fox was the headmaster at Stuart Hall during Jason's siege. He was a brilliant mind and an incredible man. He certainly had his hands full with Jason and while extremely challenged by it all, I'm sure he loved every minute of it. He would tell me later on that when Jason was in his office (and this was on quite a regular basis) that he would be stern with him but was trying all the while to suppress a giggle himself. He admired and respected Jason. This was a fact that Jason would never have believed while he was a student at the school but that he embraced and was very proud of later on. He and Father Fox became extremely close after Jason joined the Marines and corresponded frequently. Jason sought his council often while he was in Iraq and it was amusing to me to hear Jason speak of the man that he had once referred to as "The Old Blowhard" with such a degree of love and respect. He was constantly telling his fellow Marines, "Well, in the words of the wise and gracious Father Fox..."

Father Fox became seriously ill while Jason was in Iraq and Jason was terrified that something was going to happen to him before he could get home. He made me promise that if the worst were to happen to Father Fox, that I would contact the Red Cross as I had when Jason's grandfather had passed away. He needed to get home to him, even if he couldn't do it in time. Irony is often cruel. Father Fox could not have predicted that it would be he who would have attended Jason's funeral. His health had failed drastically and when we asked if he would speak at Jason's service, he agreed to do so to whatever degree he would be able. Jason's death affected him in such a profound way. In fact, the man that we saw emerge that beautiful Monday to speak on the life of my child was a man filled with both determination as well as the Holy Spirit. I believe he knew it was his Swan Song and he literally gave all he had for Jason. His words were eloquent and beautiful and his wife told me later that he had poured his heart into preparing them. She said he had labored over just the right things to say "for Jason." The man we watched before us that day was a man who floated to the podium and filled us all with what we so desperately needed and gave me a precious gift that I will hold dear always. He gave me his heartfelt words, his infinite wisdom, and most importantly, he gave himself.

Father Fox passed away just two months later. Selfishly, I felt comfort alongside my grief because I knew he was with Jason. I went into Jason's room and retrieved the copy of the words Father Fox had delivered at Jason's service. While the words themselves could never convey what was given that day with his delivery, as only he could, I would like you to know of them as best you can.

MEMORIAL SERVICE REMARKS:
JASON REDIFER
FEBRUARY 7, 2005

A Reading from the Letter of Saint Paul the Apostle to the Romans, beginning in the eighth chapter, at the thirty-first verse:

"If God is for us, who is against us? He who did not spare His own Son, but gave Him up for us all, will He not also give us, along with Him, everything else? ... Who shall separate us from the love of Christ? Shall hardship, or distress, or persecution, or famine, or nakedness, or peril, or sword? ...

No, in all these things we are more than conquerors through Him who loved us.

For I am sure that neither death, nor life, nor angels, nor rulers, nor things present, nor things to come, nor powers, nor height, nor depth, nor anything else in all creation, will be able to separate us from the love of God in Christ Jesus our Lord."

The Word of the Lord! (Thanks be to God.')

In the Name of God: Father, Son, and Holy Spirit. (Amen.)

The apostle Paul, who wrote these words to the tiny, frightened, persecuted Christian community at Rome, was not a man who harbored any illusions. At the gates of Damascus, he had been blasted off his horse by the power of Almighty God, had been confronted by the Risen Lord Himself; had been stripped of all the illusions and delusions of his former life, had been blinded so that he might begin to see, and had been made an Apostle of the Gospel- the most powerful message of love ever known to human beings. Then, for attempting to spread that Gospel throughout the entire known world, he had been ruthlessly hunted by his former friends and employers, he had been beaten up, flogged, stoned, and run out of town in virtually every city in Asia Minor, he had been shipwrecked, he had been bitten by poisonous snakes, he had been tried in kangaroo courts, he had been rejected by many of those to whom he had first given the Gospel, and he was now on his way to Rome, where he knew he was likely to be killed. Indeed, during the persecution of the Emperor Nero, Paul was beheaded by an executioner's sword - and a sword has become his symbol.

(2)

Paul was not, then, a person who believed in some Polyanna-type, touchy-feely, squishy heart version of the Gospel of Jesus Christ. He had come, through hard discipline, very realistic - and, therefore, very powerful - understanding of the Gospel. Because of how Paul had chosen to live his life, he had enormous credibility. He was, as an Apostle, "the real thing."

So, when he wrote to the Christians at Rome that he was sure that NOTHING, *not* suffering, not loss, not danger, not the executioner's beheading sword - of which he seems to have had a premonition -, not death itself - that NOTHING can separate us from the love of God manifested in Christ Jesus, he meant it. Not only did he mean it, he lived it - at whatever cost that entailed. Not only did he live it, he died for it. By dying for it, he showed that his belief in this message of absolutely reliable, immensely powerful love was a complete and total belief. To use the common vernacular, he put his money where his mouth was. He not only talked the talk; he walked the walk.

Like most all of you, I knew Jason Redifer very well. Several of the many newspaper articles that have, in recent days, attempted to tell Jason's extraordinary story and to capture his incredible person hood have mentioned that, from time to time, Jason got into scrapes with "the administration" at Stuart Hall. That would have been with me! Indeed, Jason came to my office enough times that, on arriving, he went right over to what he called "my reserved seat."

Jason never attempted to avoid responsibility for what he had done. One of his stock lines was, "Yep, I did that," followed by a quizzical shake of the head, as if to indicate "but I can't believe that I really did!" When we were finished, Jason always shook hands before he left. Nobody else did that; it was "original Jason." There was never any evasion, or beating around the bush with Jason. He was a straight shooter, who, very early in life, had attained the wonderful ability - which many of us never seem quite to reach - of being able to tell the truth about himself to himself. Like the Apostle Paul, he had no illusions. Like the Apostle Paul, Jason "spoke the truth in love." Both of them sometimes ruffled feathers!

Jason, as you all know, was a cowboy. He was a real, honest to God cowboy.

When I was a mountain guide, thirty years ago, out in Jackson Hole, Wyoming, I used to see lots of phony cowboys, who had just bought their Tony Lama boots and Stetson hats at Wyoming Outfitters - pardon me, WY-o-ming Outfitters - and who were swaggering around, jingling their pseudo-silver spurs, far out there in pseudo-cowboy fantasy land. Jason was not pseudo-anything and certainly not pseudo-cowboy. He rode horses and worked stock. He competed in the rodeo and helped pay his

Stuart Hall tuition by riding a bull or two. Jason lived by the code of the Old West. His word was his bond. He was forthright. He had a helping hand for others. Yes, he had boots and a big belt buckle, but the Way of the Cowboy was in him - not on him. He valued God, country, and family.

(3)
He believed intensely and passionately in the old-time virtues-and values that many highly refined cynics today choose to scoff at. He not only believed in them; he lived them. He had enormous credibility. He was "the real thing."
Like most of you, I could tell many stories about Jason - he has left us the gift of great stories, stories very worth remembering. Tell them; preserve them. Time is short. I'll tell just two. On Christmas Eve, 2002, the phone rang at Worthington House. It was Jason. Was I doing anything? Why, did he need something? Ah, ah, well, he had come to the school with his Marine recruiter, because - ah - you see, he needed - ah - a complete transcript, grade report, and recommendation - today, December 24th, in order to be taken into the Marine Corps on time, right after graduation, and the school was ah - closed, and ... ah ... "I'll be right over," I said. So, I went over and got all those things together, spoke with the very impressive recruiter in his dress uniform, told him what a fine young man Jason was, and, as the Scripture says, "It came to pass," and Jason did enter the Marine Corps right after Graduation, 2003. In the last week, I've thought about that Christmas Eve meeting quite a bit. Like many of you, I've had my share of "What if" thoughts.
The second story is about that last time I actually saw Jason in person. It was at Stuart Hall's Graduation, 2004. Jason had returned, a year after his own graduation, to support and to be with friends a year behind him who were graduating then. This time, it was Jason who was very impressive and in the full dress uniform. Not that Jason needed a full dress uniform to be impressive; what was impressive about him was in him, not on him. He told me about the rigors of basic training, about various things that had befallen him - for there are headmaster types - and far more! - in the Marine Corps as well - about how he had persevered, about crawling in the churned-up ooze under the barbed wire, and about how he had made it, and been inducted into the Corps. He told me how proud he was - not proud of himself or of having attained a very important goal - but proud of the Corps, proud of its tradition and its mission, proud of being, through his belonging to the Corps, part of something very important, something very worthwhile, part of a very powerful force for the right and the good. Jason believed

*that profoundly. His eyes welled up when he told me about it. That
conviction never changed. Jason testified to that same conviction in his
e-mails from Iraq. Indeed, his very presence in Iraq, when he could
instead have been part of the prestigious Honor Guard at the White
House, testified to the power of that conviction.*

*Like the Apostle Paul, Jason lived his convictions through whatever
difficulties and challenges arose. He had survived six previous attacks
with Improvised Explosive Devices. He had been wounded. Yet, as Paul
would have said, he continued "to press onward toward the goal"
because he believed so powerfully in what the United States; at its best,
and the American people, at their best, stand for - freedom from fear and
oppression, liberty of action, speech, and conscience, self-determination,
mutual respect, and a better future.*

(4)

*Like the Apostle Paul, Jason had no illusions. On his Senior Yearbook
Page, we find not only the ringing words of John F. Kennedy's Inaugural
Address, "Ask not what your country can do for you, but what you can do
for your.country," but also the grim words of Shakespeare's Julius
Caesar, "The coward dies a thousand times, the brave man, but once." In
retrospect, that quotation seems almost a premonition. Like Paul, Jason
faced the sword, and did not flinch from it. He, too, "walked the walk."
He was true to the high ideals of his Corps. He went on that last patrol
because, "My lieutenant needs me."*

*We all needed - and still need - Jason. It is hard to think of one so vital
as being gone. It is hard to think that the deeply deposited ore of
character and virtue in Jason will, now, not be fully mined, and shared
with family and friends. But Jason is not "gone." Instead, he has entered
the New Life and the Heavenly Kingdom, where he will advance in
perfect service. NOTHING, as Paul has taught us, could separate Jason
from the love of Christ and the gift of eternal life that springs from that
all-conquering love. Not suffering, not the sword, not death itself. Jason
was about to come home on leave; instead, he has been recalled to his
heavenly home - Home with a capital "H." We are not left with futile
emptiness. Instead, Jason has given us a rich bequest, the memory and
the example of a life lived to the hilt, in full accord with deeply held
convictions and principles, a life lived very much in accord with the
fundamental Christian value of sacrificial love. In a brief span, he had
come to embody so much of profound value.*

*To his family, we, who knew Jason outside his home, can testify to how
intensely he loved each of you, how proud and fond he was especially of
his younger brothers, how he wished to enfold each and every one of you*

32

in his strong arms with that powerful, protective, joyful bear hug, that so characterized him. Jason did nothing in life by half measures; certainly he did not love save by the entirety.

To his parents, we wish to testify to how highly Jason was regarded by all who knew him well- by Stuart Hall, so proud of its pioneering male graduate, among the very first of its "sons;" by all his many friends both there and everywhere else he had touched life with his special grace and being; by the Marine Corps, which had marked Jason for special distinction; by his Marine comrades, who relied upon his valor and skill; and by his country, which will inter him tomorrow at Arlington National Cemetery. How proud you must be of a valiant and faithful son! Yet, we can only guess at the intensity of your sorrow and loss, and respectfully sympathize with it. You are in our prayers and hearts and hopes, and there you shall remain. God bless you and sustain you now and in the time to come.

Jason Redifer is now enfolded in the loving arms of his Redeemer, our Lord and Savior Jesus Christ. He now serves in the Honor Guard of the Almighty God and Father.

(5)
The Holy Spirit has already breathed upon him the New and Full Life, where sorrow and suffering is no more. May Light Perpetual shine upon him.

Family and friends, even in the sharpness of your sorrow, remember that NOTHING, not even Jason's painfully premature absence from us here, can separate us from the love of God in Christ Jesus. The God Who Himself gave His only Son as a sacrifice, so that all might come within the reach of his saving embrace and have, thereby, the gift of Eternal Life, well knows the intense pain of a son's loss. He will heal the broken heart, He will lift you up on high, and, as Paul teaches, He will render you, through the transforming power of His love, more than conquerors. God is faithful and true - indeed, He is the Great Original of "Semper Fideles," always faithful. Depend upon it, take comfort in it; and find in it the peace which passeth all understanding. AMEN.
The Rev. J. Kevin Fox, Short Form, as delivered

Yes, Jason was one squared away Marine. He was one incredible man. I knew all of this and for me, there was no question. Jason belonged in Arlington.

CHAPTER 4

A VISIT FROM MAJOR MOORE

In the days immediately following Jason's burial, we received quite a few phone calls from the young Marines who had served with him and had just returned home from Iraq. It seemed so strange that they all basically came home together, even though Jason never made it for the bus ride into LeJeune.

I felt so lost the morning that we had originally been planning to leave for Camp LeJeune to welcome home the 24th MEU (Marine Expeditionary Unit). I had most everything ready in preparation for that day. I had made most of the plans and had everything I needed to celebrate their homecoming with them all. I had everything, that is, except my Marine. There would be no celebration that day for me.

The sun rose that morning and I felt that I was somehow behind schedule. There was no schedule. We were going nowhere. There was no victory waiting for us there. I could not seem to align what I had planned for and the reality of what I ended up with. I was overcome by a sense of panic. We should have been on the road hours ago. We had to get moving. The need to assemble everyone in the vehicle and blast out of the driveway consumed me. I stood in my living room literally not knowing what to do. I was again overwhelmed with loss. There was no need to gather up anything, call for anyone to hurry along, or even to go start the car. We were going nowhere. The bus would be rolling into the base in several hours bringing home weary young men fresh from battle and longing for the sight of their loved ones. Jason would not be among them. I had already seen in my mind's eye what he would look like and how he would feel and how I would hold him until my tears of joy subsided and finally how we would all celebrate! I could picture him sweeping up his younger brothers into his arms and telling them how much they had grown while he was away. He would awkwardly hug Justin and they would both fight back the tears. Scott would try to maintain a manly composure without visible emotion but would melt away into his own tears of pride and relief as they embraced. None of this would come to pass for us.

I felt so utterly isolated. I was thrown out of my universe and all that was familiar to me. I had no idea where I had landed or even how to find oxygen there.

I seriously contemplated, as I had the day before, just going on to Camp Lejeune anyway and welcoming home his unit. After all, we were proud of them and their service and were relieved that they were safely back home. Why shouldn't we be there to celebrate their victorious return just because Jason wasn't with them? Of course, how would these war-weary young men feel as they came bounding off a bus anxiously trying to catch sight of their loved ones and see, instead, the mother of one of their comrades who was just killed. Talk about a bummer. Should they not be granted a reprieve and be allowed to trade in that particular horror for a moment of joy and relief? The last thing I wanted was to impose more pain on these already tortured souls. I just wanted them to know that it was O.K.

Unfortunately, I wasn't exactly O.K.

The time passed slowly and eventually I had to accept that we would be leaving for nowhere. There would be no road trip, no welcoming committee. We were just going to stay in our house and grieve what we would not be receiving into our loving fold. Jason had already come home in the only way that he was ever going to again.

As the calls began to trickle in, I had the opportunity to speak with several of the friends that Jason had talked to me about. It was so hard to hear their pain. I knew what it must have taken for them to call me. How difficult it must have been for them, fresh from the line of duty, to call the grieving mother of someone they lost. What could they have anticipated saying to me and worse yet, what could they have dreaded hearing from me? Yet, with courage and character, they phoned.

One such call came and changed my life. The voice on the other end was of a man who would become a lifeline to me. He would become someone that I would share a connection with like no other person in my life. Jason had served under him in Iraq and he would share my loss in a way that was understood only to us. He was Major Billy Moore. His rank had advanced from Captain since his return from deployment and I could feel the newness of it in his voice. He hadn't quite settled into it yet, although I would quickly see that it suited him well.

He introduced himself and said that he wanted to come to our house to speak with us. He was headed in our direction and told me about when he expected to come through. What he didn't say was that after having been deployed for six months and having only been home with his wife and three young daughters for a matter of hours, he turned around and left them again. He had a duty to fulfill. Not a Marine's duty as a Major, but a Marine's duty as a man. It was a matter of character for him. He was taking his leave time to come and visit the three families who had lost their sons under his command and to visit the two survivors who were in serious condition at Bethesda Navy Medical Hospital.

I found myself being nervous as I anticipated his arrival. Would he view this shattered family worthy of the young Marine he had surely come to know? Would he bring me little anecdotes of Jason shining through as his unique, vibrant self from under the uniformity that was the Corps? Would he tell me tales of horror and combat or weave me yarns of the spoils of war? Far removed from any of these, and by far worse, would be a scenario where after initial pleasantries we would just sit awkwardly in the silence of death.

When he came through my front door I instantly knew him. No, he was no one I had ever met before but he was known to me just the same. He was young and handsome and fit. As it should be. He had a strong, determined jaw. I realized at that moment that the cliché is true. Eyes really are the windows to your soul. His were intense and penetrating and behind the veil of pain and despair, I could faintly see a glimpse of their steely beauty. The eyes of character, honor, humility and loyalty were cast upon me, and as I saw them flood over with tears my heart lurched and my own tears overtook me. I embraced him; clung to him as if to life itself and I believe it was at that very moment when he inherited a piece of my very being. Something sacred and foreign to anything I had ever known was born of that instant. He would become invaluable to me as he remained faithful and steadfast in his promise to never forget Jason and in his dedication to my family's well being. We would share what Jason meant to each of us in the months to come. We would trust one another with those thoughts that are often in the dark recesses of your core. We would talk about dashed hopes and disappointments, regrets and even guilt. We would share pain, joy, laughter, tears and even love. We both loved Jason–not just Lance Corporal Redifer, USMC, but the total man that Jason had become. He loved and missed my son and I knew he shared him with me in a way few others ever could. He lost him alongside of me in a way no one else would ever understand. I thought of his struggle and his demons daily in the months to come. I prayed God would grant him peace within his beautiful young family. I would meet his wife later and know immediately that all he could ever need of this Earth would be found in her loving arms. Nachelle Moore exemplifies kindness and caring and is filled with the spirit of a servant heart. It is my prayer that they will remain a part of my life forever.

During those first few minutes, however, I only knew that Major Moore would be able to bring more of Jason back home to me.

He came, in part, to do the only thing he could for the families of the fallen. "I promised my men that I would bring them all home and I failed," he said as his voice slightly cracked and he cast his eyes to the floor. I knew even as he said it that he never broke his promise to those boys. They all did come home. I also knew that he would never see it that way.

He told us everything he could that day about the overall mission, that particular ill-fated patrol and, of course, the details of the actual explosion. He could not, however, tell us the details that I know now we were not ready to hear. I think he tried to be as frank and honest with us as possible and made every effort to speak with complete candor. As he was describing the gruesome accident site, our eyes met briefly and I saw something inside him shut me out. I knew I had just been locked out of something significant, yet I dared not call him on it. Perhaps it was just not something I was prepared to deal with. I thought I needed every minute detail so that I could put as many pieces together as possible. I needed every tool I could rally to try to find some acceptance and possible closure. Yet, in the telling of that brief glance I was not certain if either of us was prepared to face the truth that was remaining undisclosed. I would leave it alone.

Later, the information that eluded me that day would come to me in its entirety and I would have more pieces than I would ever have wanted to put together. I am thankful it was not that day.

He answered all the questions we posed to him and many that we had not even had the presence of mind to formulate yet.

I had been given very little information by anyone up to this point. Of course, I have no idea exactly what was explained to me when the Casualty Assistance Calls Officers (CACO) came with the news on the day he was killed. I don't even remember actually hearing those horrible words, although I am certain I must have. I knew he was dead when I saw their presence. I didn't need the words. They obviously told us that there was an IED (improvised explosive device) explosion in the Babil Province, just south of Baghdad, in the "triangle of death" as it had been dubbed due to the casualty rate there. We knew that three Marines were dead and two seriously wounded with life threatening injuries. I was told the time of death and had the clarity to immediately count backward eight hours to convert the time to USA east coast time. I realized all too clearly that it was only two hours after I heard his voice.

Major Moore confirmed that they were on their final patrol. He said that, had they been successful, they all would have returned to the base to begin packing for their return to the United States.

I won't ever say that Jason knew he was going to die that day but he certainly knew that his danger there was not over. He had been so pleased and relieved that the Iraqi elections were over and had been a success and he felt he had been a tiny little part of that. Even surrounded in that overall euphoria he seemed very subdued about the impending mission and that was quite unlike him. No matter how tired, hurt, afraid or worried he may ever be he would never have wanted it to show through to me. He could not stand thinking about me being upset or worried for him. He told everyone he corresponded with to "please take care of Mom," "please check in on Mom" and "promise me you'll look after Mom."

I have heard many reports, stories, and tales regarding the events of that fateful day. Many accounts have indicated that Jason should not have even been in that Humvee. One such story told to me said that Jason had just returned from an all night duty elsewhere, with another group. He would often go on "guardian angel"patrols. Basically guarding over other groups of service members while they were engaged in various missions. This was said to have been the case the night before the accident. I was told that when he discovered that his group was going on patrol, he insisted in joining them. I think anyone who has ever been in a combat situation can understand that loyalty to "your boys" was far more important to you than sleep. He was granted permission and then the tale is further picked up by Staff Sergeant Lorenzetti who told me that Jason was to have been his driver for that day. I know Jason was often the driver on missions and that morning he pleaded with Staff Sergeant Lorenzetti to be allowed to go in the other Humvee with his buddies. The Staff Sergeant didn't immediately agree but finally relented since it was their final patrol. Jason ended up being the front passenger in the Humvee that was hit. The driver of their vehicle was Lance Corporal Harry Swain, Jason's good friend who had been given the responsibility of contacting me should something happen to Jason. After I received the news on January 31st, I waited to hear from Harry. The call never came.   I eventually realized that he too had perished.

There were three other Marines in the back of the vehicle: Corporal Christopher Zimny (who was also killed), Lance Corporal Jamel Daniels (who was blown upward 35 feet through the turret) and Lance Corporal Ron Howard (who was blown out of the vehicle laterally).

While in Iraq, Lance Corporal Jamel Daniels had a wife, Jessica and a son, five-year-old Jamel Jr., home in New York. He later described the last patrol in his own words: *"We were told on the night of January 30th, 2005 that our squad would be going out on our last patrol the following morning. We got up early, had breakfast and I went over to the Computer Center before we had a briefing on the mission. Our Platoon Staff Sergeant Lorenzetti and Squad Leader Sergeant Augustine gave us about a 20-minute briefing and then we checked our weapons, ammo and water supply before mounting up in our vehicles. We were happy and joking around as we loaded up. Happy that this would be our last patrol. We were to go home in just twelve days. There were five guys in my Humvee. Lance Corporal Harry Swain was driving, Lance Corporal Jason Redifer in the front passenger seat, Lance Corporal Ron Howard behind him and Corporal Christopher Zimny in the back seat behind the driver. I was manning the M249 in the turret. We were all real good friends. We were in a convoy of four Humvees. We were in the second Humvee as we rode out and did our mission, then turned around and started back. The first vehicle had passed by this hidden IED and when we reached the spot, it was detonated. It went off in a flash. I was blown straight up in the air some thirty-five feet. I was conscious when I was in the air but I don't remember landing, apparently I had blacked out for a few seconds. I remember coming to in the crater made by the sixteen 155mm shells that had been set off directly under our vehicle. I was in pain and shock but I couldn't feel anything below my waist. I was crying and was thinking what the hell just happened. I saw Lance Corporal Stevens and Lance Corporal McMahon running over to me. They began giving me aid. The other three Humvees had set up a defensive perimeter around the explosion area. Corpsman HM3 Allen ran over and began giving me aid. He told me my buddies were all dead. I was thinking I was going to die and I was worried about what would happen to my wife and small son. They called in a QRF (Quick Reaction Force) to come and assist us. What was left of our vehicle began to cook off with the ammo and grenades that were in the Humvee. I learned later that Lance Corporal Howard had also survived.*

Editors note. Lance Corporal Jamel Daniels lost a leg and would spend over a year in the hospital recuperating from the violent explosion.

The explosion occurred directly beneath Jason's seat.

The "what ifs," "I should haves," and "if onlys," will only serve to make us all insane. The bottom line is that God put Jason exactly where he needed to be that day for the plan that He has. Can I even begin to rationalize that or understand it? Of course not! I must simply accept that it is something far greater than I will ever be able to comprehend while on this Earth. I must just trust in my faith or let myself die in the pursuit of all the "whys."

The patrol consisted of four vehicles and Jason was in the second or third in line. The group was driving around a hole in the road that was created from a previous IED explosion. Someone, somewhere sat in wait, watched the first vehicle clear the hole, coordinated their timing and then detonated a grouping of explosives that had been buried beneath the road's surface directly alongside the previous hole. The enemy knew that this road would eventually have to be used again and the now limited remaining surface area made ripe this spot for murder. Jason's vehicle was an up-armored Humvee and still managed to be decimated.

Some unseen enemy, far from the view of those whom he targeted, simply dialed a cell phone or pushed a remote control and blew three of America's finest into their eternity and left two others wishing they were dead. This was the largest IED explosion in that region to date.

My questions concentrated mainly on the condition of Jason's body. The CACO officers had to tell me during

"Phase II" that the report from Dover indicated that Jason's body would be "unviewable." Due to the nature of the accident, I deciphered this to mean that my child would be coming home to me in pieces.

Those bastards killed my son in a cowardly, gutless manner and then stole from me even my ability to say goodbye. "Phase II" ended that day with a request for my signature on a form that basically made me aware that he would, in fact, return home in parts.

"Phase III" kicked off the next day with yet another form to sign. This one basically made notice that I was correct, and since Jason would only be returning in segments, I was aware it would therefore be impossible to even retrieve all of those. Of course, I knew everything that could physically be seen and claimed would be gathered and handled with the utmost respect. The facts remained.

Finally, I had to indicate my decision regarding whether or not I would require notification should any further remains be discovered at some future point in time. I could only envision a small group of Iraqi children playing in the sand, chasing a ball, perhaps, when they would stumble onto something that would turn out to be Jason's head! Would someone be dispatched to I.D. it? Would it then be boxed up and "FedEx'd "back to the states? Would handsome young Marines be again sent to my home with another round of "we regret to inform you..." I remember thinking that I could quite possibly throw up. Amazingly, I did not.

I asked Major Moore, while in my living room, if he had been able to recognize Jason at all. I needed to know just how he determined it was him. He stumbled through fragments of thoughts and words and finally, he emphatically indicated to me that with certainty he knew it was Jason.

I was terribly confused. I wondered if Jason's body had simply been burned beyond recognition in the fire that resulted after the initial explosion. Major Moore had said that they had difficulty approaching the vehicle because of the chain reaction explosions that continued after the initial blast. I thought that perhaps sometime after he had made the identification, fire had consumed him.

That was not what had happened. Jason was not burned to that degree. Again, I would not know this for some time.

The funeral home was given instructions that I was to be allowed to see my son "if there was as much as a fingernail" left of him. Even that would grant some peace to a mother who had nothing else to cling to. I understood that it was their duty to protect the ignorant families who thought they knew what was best but had no idea what they would be seeing. I talked at length to the director to be certain that he understood that I would need to be the one to make that decision and that no one was to decide that for me. I left our conversation feeling that I had been understood. I trusted that my wishes would be carried out. I was wrong.

The day we learned Jason's body had returned to the states and was at Dover Air Force Base, Delaware, I celebrated having him back on his own soil. He was away at war no more. I went upstairs and dug out from my drawer a T-shirt that my sister had given me. Jason's formal Marine picture was emblazoned on the front with a caption that read, "Part of my heart is in Iraq." I took the shirt outside and had Scott douse it with gasoline. I set fire to it and watched it burn. My heart was no longer in Iraq. He was home.

The funeral home called after they had received the body to let me know he had arrived. It was very, very difficult having to hear your child being referred to as "the body." I was promised that he would be examined and if there would be anything recognizable in his remains that I would be given a detailed description so that I could decide if I still wanted to view him. There would be no great decision for me. I needed to hold my baby, whatever that would mean.

We arrived at the funeral home and were given the news. Upon examination, they had concurred with Dover and determined the remains were not viewable. I was told that I would recognize nothing as human. After I composed myself, I tried desperately to be as rational as possible. After much agonizing, I decided that if I truly could find nothing that was my Jason that I would only be setting myself up for a horror that would surely haunt me for the rest of my days. I relented. I gave in. I sold out. I trusted and lost. I have regretted it ever since and that is now what will haunt me.

We were allowed to go into the room where he had been placed for receiving friends and family. I was allowed to open the casket with assistance from the director, after being briefed on what we would and would not see. A Marine guard was standing on duty faithfully by the casket. I was so relieved that Jason had not been all alone. The casket was draped with the beautiful flag of our country. Jason was now a part of that flag and all that it stood for. It was gently folded back and I helped lift the top of the casket open. Lying underneath was a perfect dress blue uniform of the United States Marine Corps. It had been placed on top of layers of sheeting and a blanket that covered the remains of what was my son. It was not the uniform that Jason had insisted I have dry cleaned the day before he left. It was one that had been provided by Dover. We didn't know that day that his actual uniform would not be used in case of the worst. I had tried to give it to the Casualty Officers that day but they informed me that it wouldn't be necessary.

The blazer was positioned where it would have been in relation to the casket should an actual body have been lying inside and wearing it. The brass buckle on the crisp white belt at the waist reflected my face as my salty tears flooded onto it. Upset that I had ruined its shine and luster, I tried to wipe away the smudges and make it shine again. The Marine guard, who was now the only other person in the room, whispered, "I'll take care of it, Ma'am." I heard the tremble in his voice and turned to see a single tear roll down his cheek. He was a Marine. He had lost one of his own. I would whisper back, "Semper Fi" to him later and kiss him gently on the cheek as I made my way out.

I rubbed the chest area of the blazer softly as I sobbed for the many losses I felt. When I could hold the storm inside no longer, I leaned over the casket and placed my arms inside, sliding my hands under whatever was wrapped up in that covering. I held that bundle as close to my being as I could. I squeezed tightly and held on. I pretended in my mind that it was the hug I had longed to embrace him with upon his safe return. I have no comprehension of how long I just hung over the side of that casket and held my baby to my breast. I just held him as tightly to me as I could and I held him and I held him, and I held him.

When I could no longer physically hold myself up, after crying myself into exhaustion, I released him for what I knew would be the last time.

I had an opportunity to open his casket one final time while it was resting in the church, the night before the funeral. Scott, Justin and I took all the things we had gathered that we wanted placed inside with him. A friend of the boys had pulled hair out of Jason's horse's mane and had woven it into a pattern for him. We placed it inside so his precious ones would always be with him. Courtland and Carter had each drawn pictures and had their own little mementos to go inside. We put in his favorite John Wayne movie ("McClintock") and other odds and ends that we felt he would "want along for the ride." Lastly, we placed his cowboy hat on what should have been his chest.

When we were finished, I tucked the silky, ruffled material in around him like a mother tucks her newborn baby into a bassinet and I said to him, "from the cradle to the grave, Son." I closed the lid forever. I was given the special key that locks it shut and with a sturdy turn he was prepared for his eternal rest.

I looked around at all of the mementos and photos of Jason that surrounded his casket. I looked at a pair of his combat boots that were on one side with a helmet and flak jacket. On the other side was his old pair of cowboy boots, an old cowboy hat and a fishing pole. I was glad he would be resting there in God's house for the night. I could never have left him in a funeral home.

I inquired from Major Moore, before he left from his visit, about the survivors of the accident. I was concerned about their condition and didn't know if he would be allowed to give out that kind of information on them or not. He told me that they were at Bethesda Naval Medical Center and partially described their injuries.

I knew that I had missed my opportunity to go to Camp LeJeune and welcome home the troops but I would not miss a new opportunity to go to these fine men. I decided immediately that I would leave the following day for Maryland.

Before Major Moore would "take his leave" I gave him something very special to me. It was a photograph taken of Jason on his favorite horse just before he left for Iraq. The picture was taken by Julie Dodd, a professional photographer who was in one of our fields one evening photographing a century old house which had stood empty for years. Just as she was shooting, a dust cloud rose up and over the hill appeared Jason. She thought the scene was beautiful as it was just about sundown and she took a whole series of shots. She enjoyed them so much that she displays one in her gallery and has named it "Joy Ride." I was honored when she brought me a copy after he had gone overseas. He never had the chance to see it but he would have treasured it. That photograph was "Jason." It is a black and white silhouette of him riding off into the sunset. That is exactly how Jason would have wanted to be remembered.

CHAPTER 5

BETHESDA

The following morning I went to Maryland. I desperately needed to see the Marines who had shared in this horrific accident with my son. This was going to connect me to it all. Up until now it had been my own private Hell. Now, I would enter a zone where it would be shared with the others who were being held prisoner there. I needed desperately to see them. I needed to hold them and tell them how thankful I was that they were alive. I needed to let them know that I celebrated their homecoming. I needed them to know how much I ached for them and how sorry I was that they had experienced such unimaginable evil. I needed them to not feel guilty to have survived. I needed them to see something of Jason and to know that it would be O.K. I needed all of these things for them but perhaps, most of all; I just needed to be with them.

My mother and sister-in-law went along to support me, to support these two young men and probably to fill their own need as well. We left, fully loaded, with gifts, snacks and homemade cards for each. We took flowers and balloons and everything we could think of to try to make them more comfortable. It was difficult to know what the appropriate protocol required here. I was so anxious to see them and became even more determined as the miles ticked off behind us.

This could not, I decided, be about my grief. I may have needed something from them but I was going to do everything I could to remain positive and focus on helping them heal. I could fall apart once we were back in the car, if necessary. I was going to take strength to them, not weakness. I would deliver healing, not destruction.

It wasn't until we had parked the car and were getting out that I thought about it. What if they wouldn't want to see me? What if they couldn't or wouldn't face the mother of their war brother who was slain? What kind of position would I be putting them in to force them to have to come up with even something to say to me?

I thought about it all for a moment and then remembered Major Moore's voice as he described their injuries to me and also their emotional state. Lance Corporal Jamel Daniels, the Marine who had been manning the turret, had already had one leg amputated and would possibly be losing the other. He had emergency surgery in Germany before being flown to Bethesda and would later tell me that he remembered very little before waking up to discover that he was in a hospital in the U.S. and that three of his friends had not survived. He knew the only other survivor was just down the hall but was unable to see him for days. The only memory he would be able to recount to me prior to that was of being pushed violently into the air in a tuck position. He had many other relatively serious injuries but none as much as those to his legs.

Lance Corporal Ron Howard had been literally blown out of the Humvee along with a side door that he had buckled himself to. As it turned out, strapping himself to it with the seat belt, in an attempt to hold the broken door shut, turned out to be what was attributed to saving his life. His injuries were many and varied too and Major Moore told us that his jaw had been broken and was wired shut.

I decided to say a quick prayer and go on inside. I had explained to the guard at the hospital entrance gate that I was the mother of a Marine who had just been killed in Iraq and that I was there to visit the accident survivors. Obviously shaken by my announcement, he directed us to the appropriate entrance. He informed me that I should report to the Marine Liaison office once inside and I was doing exactly that. In this office, I reported the same information to the Marine on desk duty and instantly additional Marines were dispatched to assist us. They carried all the gift-wrapped presents we had as well as the balloons and flowers. They escorted us to the floor where Jamel and Ron were being cared for. When we arrived outside of Jamel's room, one of the Marines started to go inside and make sure it was suitable for us to enter. I asked that he announce us and tell Jamel who I was so that he might have the opportunity to voice any opposition to allowing me in. I was announced and welcomed in. Jamel's grandmother was standing at the foot of his bed and we would learn that she had not left his side since he was flown in. When I saw his precious face, I knew I had made the right decision in coming. In fact, I believe now that God sent me there. Jamel opened his arms to me and when I went to him he held me and we cried together. So much for keeping a stiff upper lip, Rhonda! We stayed that way for a long time, clinging to something precious. We were trying to pull each other to safety. I moved back slightly after a long while so that I could look into his eyes. With our faces close to one another, I whispered softly to him that I would absolutely NOT allow him to feel guilty for coming home alive. I told him that we would deal with this loss together and that God obviously had a plan for him that he had yet to complete. I reminded him that we often don't know what it is that we're supposed to be doing but that his very survival was evidence that God controls all.

I told him how proud I was of him and how thankful I was that he was home. I promised that he would not have to bear this journey to recovery alone. I told him that I loved him. We talked for a long time and he held onto me as if he never wanted to let go. His injuries were bad and I felt a huge lump in my throat when he showed me what was now a stump and said simply, "I miss my leg." He said it like a child would remark of a beloved family dog that was lost. It was humbling.

We were eventually able to share a little joy that day as a relationship unlike any other I had ever forged had been born. The intensity could have easily overcome me. I left his room that day knowing two things: that I would soon return; and that two people who loved Jason now loved one another. That love was about to encompass one more.

When I entered Ron's room the first thing I saw was a set of blue eyes that were almost electric with brilliant color. Then, I saw them fill and spill over with tears and by the time I reached his bedside he was holding out a broken arm, trying to reach for me. Though his jaw was forced shut he kept trying to speak through clenched teeth. "I'm so sorry. I'm so sorry." He uttered it over and over again as though he was both confessing and begging for absolution. "I'm so sorry." He was broken and he was broken for me. I held him and rocked him like a child. I told him the same things I had told Jamel about God's plan and begged him to let go of the guilt. He looked at me with the same devastated look I had just seen two doors down and I knew that even though they wanted nothing more, they would never leave it behind.

Many months later, when Lance Corporal Ron Howard was no longer hospitalized, I received an email from him that read: *"Jason was a person that would help you in every way possible. The friendship that I had with him was that of a brother.*

Ron has also written numerous entries on memorial sites that have listed Jason's death. The following two were around Christmas 2005, our first Christmas without Jason:

"I met Red (Jason) about two years ago in infantry school. We were in the same company there and when we got to fleet, we were in the same company, same platoon and the same squad. Red was a great person. You could count on him cracking jokes just to make us laugh. He was the greatest friend anyone could have. I loved working with him because he was the one to keep you awake, when needed. I was in the same accident with him. I suffered some serious injuries but am recovering well. I was in deep pain when I found out about his death. I just cried. That is all I could do. His family was great. They came and visited me and the other person who was seriously injured, also. I want to send my deepest sympathy to them around this time of the year and I also want them to know I pray for them and Jason every night."

"Jason, man, I miss you very much. It is not the same without you anymore, or Swain or Zimny, but me, you and the gang had great times. I just want you to know that I think about you all the time. Your are a one of a kind friend. To the family of Red: I want to thank you.

You have been there for me and Jamel. We both cared so much about Jason because he was a great friend and you are all one of a kind. I have never met people that care so much for people. That is great. I love you all. You are like my family now. You are in my heart. I want you, the family, to stay strong and believe for me." Lcpl Ronald Howard, 1/2 Alpha Co. 24th MEU of Bethesda Maryland National Naval Medical Center.

Ron and Jamel were very different young men with very individual personalities, lives and even injuries. Yet, we were three lost wanderers, of one heart, on a voyage that only we could travel now. I knew that a part of each of them had died with the news of that day as well.

Leaving that hospital was very difficult that day. We would try to say our good-byes but we just couldn't seem to pull away from each other. The closer I would get to the door, the smaller they would seem lying there in their beds. They were so helpless, physically and emotionally. Ron, with his broken and wired jaw, was so limited in communicating except with his azure eyes. Jamel, with one leg completely missing and facing the uncertainty of the fate of the other, was unable to communicate much of what was inside him as well. I don't think they had any idea what was there. They just knew it was a dark, horrifying place that they were praying to be delivered from.

They both had enormous contraptions encircling their lower legs, ankles and feet. These "halos" held steel rods that pierced through the skin, through the bones and resurfaced on the other side. They were of varying sizes and were used to keep the areas intact while fusion of the broken bones inside could hopefully take place.

I likened this to holding the reassembled pieces of a broken toy together while the SuperGlue dried. Sometimes the repairs worked and your toy was fixed. Sometimes the glue would dry and would appear to hold the repairs until the toy was played with the next time. Of course, there were also times when the mess was just too great to even hold together at all.

I believe the pieces were reassembled as best they could be and then everyone held on and prayed for the miracle of the "glue." The doctors were trying what they could and hoping their patients would again be able to play.

Jamel would ultimately be the one to remain in the halo the longest at almost a year. They could not walk or even turn themselves over in bed while they were pinned in this way.

They were broken in all the ways a man can be and I almost couldn't bear walking away and leaving them behind. They were both suffering from nightmares of the accident when they could sleep. And facing the real life nightmare of the accident when they were awake.

I believe this was the first time in my life that I recognized what I believed to be a calling from God. I felt he reached inside my pain and pulled me forward to act. He sent me to Bethesda that day, for me and for Jamel and Ron. He sent me for them. He sent me for me.

When I did leave, I felt a tugging at my heart that reminded me of how I felt leaving Arlington after Jason's burial.

I hadn't really talked to Jamel and Ron about Jason's funeral or burial. We mainly spoke of him as he was in life. After all, these men had not been able to process him as dead yet.

As I was fighting back that consuming feeling on the way home, I thought back to when I had first felt it.

We rode to Arlington along with about two hundred and fifty other people on February 08, 2005. It was the day following Jason's funeral. Two full charter busses full of mourners, along with numerous private passenger vehicles made the journey to lay to rest my baby boy.

The church had overflowed the previous day for the funeral, so I was surprised that the burial service drew so many. This was a Tuesday! These people had jobs that they needed to be at!

The Stuarts Draft Veterans of Foreign Wars paid for one of the busses and Calvary United Methodist Church, which we were members of, paid for the other. The Quick-Livick Bus Company provided the busses at cost in appreciation for Jason's service to our country.

We were told that the graveside service would be brief and I hoped that all of these people would not be disappointed to have made such a journey for such a short ceremony.

When we arrived, the enormity of the history and honor engulfing the place simply blanketed me. I tried to steel myself as I watched Jason's casket being removed from the hearse and carried toward the gravesite. I knew this was it. He was going before me for the very last time. I fell into step behind the Marines carrying him and followed them to our chairs. We were seated just in front of that horrible hole in the ground. The honor guard moved as one flawless unit, every step, every breath, in sync.

The folding of the flag was an event in its own right. I remember feeling like the world was somehow suspended in time as each maneuver was executed to perfection. The firing of the rifles jolted my being with both the sound and the symbolism. A lone bugle sang out "Taps." So lonely and empty, the tune cried its mournful notes and the agonizing melody settled over our raw, bleeding spirit. It sang of the setting sun on my son's life. Then, silence. Loud, unbearable silence screamed out.

The weather was a freakishly balmy, sunny February day. I wasn't even wearing a sweater and I remember that in this seemingly eternal moment of silence, I felt the sun warm on my face in a way I had never before felt. It was the light of Heaven, I decided, opening up for my Jason.

My next awareness was of the flag being presented to me. Surreal. I remember thinking it was all surreal. I was on the outside looking in. I was watching this cinematic event being acted out on the silver screen and I was just an audience observer. I watched the script unfolding until I was snapped back by a harsh reality. I began to hear words audibly and my eyes cleared until I could crisply see another's eyes and I began to feel the gravity of the fact. I was, at that moment, the mother you see on TV wearing the oversize, dark sunglasses and dressed all in black, accepting the folded American flag. I was not in black, however. I was in pinstripes with a bright fuchsia blouse and was holding my unobscured face toward the sun. I had chosen my ensemble in honor of Jason's life, not in mourning for Jason's death. He was vibrant and alive and my splash of vivid color was to remind me that this vitality would live on in us all.

I was now hearing the words being given to me but the Marine delivering them was conveying so much more than he could have known. I would later learn that his name was Marine Gunnery Sergeant Barry Baker and that our brief but poignant moment together would be memorialized in a photograph that would be seen around the world. He reached out and held me, even though he appeared to be only offering his words and a flag. Sometime during that presentation, his heart embraced mine and I saw it all unfold on his face. I fought back an overwhelming urge to just throw my arms around him and release my sobs. I ended up simply reaching up to touch his cheek. I didn't think about it. I just did it. I could have sat like that forever, just keeping my hand on this empathetic man who on this day in Hell became my angel. It was never about the words he uttered. It was the song of his heart.

Suddenly, all too quickly, it was over. The end. It was finished. Time to go. Time to let the ceremonies conclude and embrace the finality of the moment. Scott, Courtland and Carter had dug up some dirt from the hill on the farm that was Jason's favorite place to ride his horse. They had bagged it the night before and brought it along to sprinkle in his grave. They scattered it gently into that horrible opening in the ground. Jason would now always have a little bit of the home he loved so dearly with him for eternity.

I tried to find some comfort in that as I was led past the casket for a final review. I placed my single flower on top. It was just a burial box now. It was no longer adorned with our country's colors and even though the beauty of the wood gleamed in that warm sunshine, it was one of the most horrible things I had ever looked upon.

Scott gently pulled me toward the bus and I boarded quickly and took my seat. I looked out my window to see my child's casket sitting there, all alone. It was just there balanced above the ground, waiting to be lowered into the dirt after we would drive away. It stood out in such sharp contrast to the white uniformity of the marble stones. Jason was there, just outside this bus and I was going to simply drive away and leave him all alone. Alone, so far from home, so far from me.

The bus began to pull away and I pushed myself against the glass. I wanted desperately to scream out and run back. We made a series of three right-hand turns to return to the road we came in on and drive toward the cemetery exit. We made a complete box around the section of lawn where he sat. I viewed that lone casket in the middle of that piece of burial ground from every conceivable direction and I didn't think I would survive leaving him behind. I quickly and frantically sent up a prayer that God would just take my life right then and there. "Hurry please, before we reach Memorial Bridge." A just Lord would bring me home before I would have to bear this too.

I abandoned my son. I cast him away like he was truly now just a box of something dead that I left in that field to rot. I did that horrible thing and God made me live through it.

We pulled further and further away as I stretched further and further back trying to keep him in my sight through that window. When we had driven completely out of the cemetery, I lowered my hand from the window and melted in my seat, defeated. The bus was completely silent. I wondered if they could all hear my soul screaming out.

On my exit from Bethesda Naval Hospital after my visit that day, I felt like I was leaving behind two more sons. If God could still love me at all, he would let me return for these.

CHAPTER 6

THE FUNERAL

Jason's funeral had been an amazing event. Of course, there was unbearable grief and loss but there had also been unheralded rejoicing in a life that had touched so many. The sanctuary had been filled with videos, photographs, mementos and personal belongings that exemplified Jason's purpose and life. He was many things inside of one nineteen year old being.

So many friends who considered Jason a part of their families, worked diligently to memorialize Jason's life in ways that would honor him, represent the ideals that he believed in and remind us all of what we would be without in his passing.

Upon my request, the U.S. Marine Corps displayed crossed American and U.S. Marine Corps flags. One side of his casket represented Jason, the Marine. A pair of combat boots, a flak jacket and a Kevlar vest adorned a wooden cross. The other side represented Jason, the man. A pair of riding chaps, a pair of old work gloves, a fishing pole and a pair of beaten up cowboy boots were placed all about a rocking chair. I could just see him rocking away, flashing that smile and yelling out, "Howdy!" to everyone that happened by.

The music was played, as requested by Jason. "God Bless the USA" was a song that was made famous by Lee Greenwood and was performed by Brent Pirkey, an amazing musical talent from our area. Brent didn't know us but answered a call for help when we needed someone to try to tackle this difficult song. "The Dance" recorded by Garth Brooks, was performed by our church's own "Harmony Hill" group. A member of that group, Dennis Claytor, also blessed us with his version of "Go Rest High on that Mountain" which had been written and recorded by Vince Gill. Jason felt these songs were filled with the messages and spirit that he believed in and had made sure to designate them on the "instructions" he left for me.

My mother's minister, Rev. David Burch, offered us words of comfort and our own minister, Rev. B. Failes, Jr. delivered the sermon. Father J. Kevin Fox provided words of grace. Jason's life was witnessed further by three people who were also very special in his life.

Brad Arnold was Jason's Military History teacher at Stuart Hall. Jason respected Mr. Arnold greatly and looked to him often for direction of character. He felt that perhaps Mr. Arnold, of all people, understood his calling to service. I think he was right. It was for this reason that I asked Mr. Arnold to speak as a representation of the honor in one's country and pride in serving, that they both felt. He was eloquent and profound.

Carole Shriver wore many hats at Stuart Hall and was involved with Jason on many levels. I believe Jason often looked to her as a moral compass, so it was within the aspect of Jason's spiritual side that I asked Carole to speak. I knew that of everyone we heard that day that she would have the most difficulty getting through it. She absolutely stunned all of those who know her by not only rising to the occasion to speak but by honoring us all in her presentation.

Lastly, Timothy Farley was once again called upon by our family. Tim and his family are simply an extension of ours. I have looked to them for guidance, acceptance, love and support on numerous occasions and they have always been there in any way needed. This was to be no exception. They met Justin and Jason when the boys were just six and four years old and had loved them ever since. Scott had the fortune of knowing Tim for the majority of his life and had always considered Tim's family as his own. I was fortunate enough to inherit them when Scott came into my life. They alone would have been reason enough to keep him!

I had called upon Tim to speak on behalf of that part of Jason that was family. Tim had dutifully served as Godfather to all my sons. He would be the voice that we could not have. Tim as expected, dutifully accepted the task. In doing so, he managed to draw something out of me that I would not have believed possible at the time. He would be honored to speak about Jason, whom he loved, but it was important to him that he also be able to take "my Jason" to those in attendance as well. He asked me to write down a few things about Jason that perhaps not everyone would know. Feeling like I had absolutely nothing left inside of me, I told him that I was certain I could not and hoped he would prepare something without me. That night before going to bed he told me that I just needed to sleep on it and see if anything came to me.

I awakened at 2:30am with a thought burning in my mind. Not even a complete thought, more like a fragment, I wrote it down just in case. After all, maybe I would be able to make something out of it for Tim, come morning. About 45 minutes later, I sat up and reached again for the pen. Another fragment. This continued until Scott suggested that I stop turning the light on and off like a cheap hotel sign and just sit up and write.

I began and when I finished, I knew that I had completed my assignment like a good student and that come morning I would please my professor. He wouldn't have to say, "I told you so." He would just give me that look of satisfaction that surely must come from knowing that you have once again helped elevate someone to find a piece of themselves that they were lacking.

Tim spoke beautifully at the service and then delivered "my Jason" to those in attendance. He read what I had written. He read my words that only he knew I had inside.

A Mother's Sweet Memories:
Jason quoted both Shakespeare and David Allen Coe
Jason loved Patsy Cline and Broadway musicals, but he did not care for cats so much
Jason always wanted an El Camino but he settled for a four-door sedan so he would have room for his future children
Jason kept photos of his family taped inside his Kevlar helmet
Jason put a steering wheel spinner on a Honda Civic

Jason rode bulls and was amazed by butterflies
Jason loved his bathrobe
Jason believed the best tales were told over coffee
Jason once went through the Arby's drive-thru on a horse
Jason once let the Stuart Hall girls shave his head with a ladies razor during school
Jason would rather work with the cows than drive a tractor on the farm
Jason always wanted to spend Christmas morning milking with Scott
Jason made sure that preschoolers and nursing home residents felt the thrill of a visit from Santa
Jason always got sick at the beach and the Olive Garden
Jason once thought artichokes were small fish
Jason was once caught by his Granddad singing, "Man, I feel like a woman"
Jason wrote out his funeral requests before he left, just in case
Jason refused to acknowledge anything but character in a man
Jason taught the local Iraqis to say, "Howdy Ya'll"
Jason spent his only "limo" ride standing up through the sunroof with his brother going through Times Square
Jason couldn't hunt but learned to see human eyes at the end of a scope
Jason would not tolerate a lifted hand to a woman; any hand, any woman
Jason never stopped kissing his father, even in public
Jason was the first person to hold his newborn brother and helped the nurse give him his first bath
Jason once asked for a sonogram picture of his younger brother to give to the school bus driver
Jason sat alone with his Grandfather's casket for four hours when he knew no one else would be there
Jason spent hours playing Canasta with his Grandmother
And Jason always brought his mother wild mustard and buttercups

The presentation of the Purple Heart followed shortly thereafter. The command was issued and every uniformed military member in attendance was on their feet and at attention. It was powerful and significant. It was overwhelming when I looked up to realize that

Justin was one of those members. He stood, face to face, with the Marine officer who was reading the citation and making the presentation in posthumous honor for his fallen brother. He stood, steeled with honor and pride and respect. He gave regard to the sacrifice of all those who have been awarded this honor prior to this day and he gave in kind for his little brother for whom he grieved. I have been proud of my oldest son on far too many occasions to count, but I was truly honored to be his mother on this day.

All too quickly, even though it had lasted about ninety minutes, the service ended. Rev. B. had come forward and placed his hand on the casket and offered a final prayer. When I opened my eyes the Marine Honor Guard began rolling the casket down the isle. I had given no thought to this portion of the program and I was panicked by it. I wanted to reach out and grab the casket and stop them from taking him away. I wanted to fall onto the floor and scream. I wanted to die. "No, wait! I'm not ready to let him go!"

I could hear the Marine Corps Hymn playing over my sobs and as I clung to Scott for what seemed like my very life, a thundercloud of emotion erupted inside of me and all that I had managed to keep in check publicly began to spill out everywhere.

Scott and Courtland practically carried me down the aisle while I felt like I was chasing Jason's casket, trying to save him from death. I was trying to keep him from going away. Carter was coming alongside, unable to know fully what was expected of him and being thrown into uncertainty as he saw his mother crumble.

Justin, I knew, was following behind with his father and I hoped they arrived in time to keep Jason from being taken.

By the time the sunlight of the newly opened door hit my face I realized that it was truly over. I had lost Jason. He would go away now.

I watched them load him into the hearse. They were precise, proud and almost mechanical in their movements. It would have been amazing to watch had they not been taking away my child. I just felt myself melting into the sidewalk like the wicked witch that Dorothy had just doused with water.

There was no procession to follow as we were not going to a cemetery at that time. The burial would not take place until the following day. So, I just watched them drive him away to the funeral home. I would be able to let him go there now. Now, he was dead.

The entire church began to flood out behind us and I thought for a moment we may be carried away by the wave. I looked at Scott, almost imploring him to just let me fall and not make me address these wonderful people who were coming to sustain me.

I knew the women of our church had a feast prepared waiting in the social hall and I knew for the first time since I was given the news that I could not face anymore. I simply could not accept greetings, well wishes, sympathy, regret, love, anything. I was spent. I begged Scott to just take me home. He encouraged me and held me up and helped me acknowledge those who came to us. Every time I felt I could draw breath no longer, he would breathe for me and keep me standing. He was my puppet master and as long as he would not let go I would keep dancing.

Eventually, I was put into a friend's car that had been brought around for us and Scott drove us home. It had been one full week since that horrific meeting of Marines in my driveway and I was mentally, physically, spiritually and emotionally exhausted.

I gave instructions once I had crawled into bed that Scott was not allowed to let anyone, other than those I had given birth to, upstairs to see me. I would do whatever necessary to be there as best I could for my sons, but I could not face another soul.

Courtland, who was just eight years old, had been leveled by the news at first but was holding up well. He stepped into manhood and began to take care of those around him. He reminded me so much of Justin. Justin and I had not yet had a chance to grieve together, nor would we for a very long time. His father was basically alone and so Justin stayed with him throughout. While at my house, he took care of people, business and anything else that needed caring for. Missy, his wife, handled everything that came in the door and stayed busy trying to keep it all straight.

Carter, being just six years old was completely unsure of what to do with the news. He seemed to just file it along with the other great mysteries of life and rolled along with whatever the agenda of the day dictated. It would be months later before he would initiate his own conversations about any of it and begin to sort things out.

We were all up early the next morning headed for Arlington.

When we returned from his burial, I scarcely had enough energy to make my way to the bed. I knew that sleep would again elude me but my body could no longer hold me. I was physically unable to keep going. Scott was trying to help me up the stairs when I heard it. A voice was calling to me from our family room. I stopped and listened and heard our President. I asked everyone to be quiet and somehow made my way to the television. We all listened as the President delivered the State of the Union Address and I was transformed. When it was over, I ascended the stairs, climbed into bed and slept until the morning.

When I awoke at six o'clock, I went immediately to my typewriter and began hammering on the keys with great intensity. Scott came in from the barn and asked what I was doing. I mumbled that I was writing a letter to the President of the United States.

"Of course you are," he replied. He then went on to make sure that everyone else in the household left me alone until I had finished my task.

The loud strikes of the keys as I banged away my message were therapeutic. I don't know why I decided to use the typewriter instead of my computer, but it was very satisfying. I typed as quickly as I could. The thoughts were simply pouring out of my soul.

When I was finished, I pulled the letter out, announced that I had written a rough draft of a letter I wanted to send to the President and then began to read it aloud to my family. When I looked up at the end, they were all staring at me as though I had grown three heads. I decided at that point that it would just be good enough as it was. I mailed it at noon.

My letter read:

February 09, 2005

President George W. Bush
The White House
1600 Pennsylvania Avenue NW
Washington, DC 20500

Dear Mr. President,

I am sending you this letter as a card of thanks. You were my son's Commander In Chief as well as his President. I am the mother of Lance Corporal Jason C. Redifer, USMC, who died on January 31, 2005 in the Babil Province of Iraq as a result of an IED explosion that ripped through the Humvee that he was in.

Jason was scheduled to return from his tour of duty in Iraq just nine days after the accident that claimed his life. He had just departed on his final mission and was killed only two hours after speaking with me on the phone. He was but a new nineteen-year-old, yet an old soul in many ways.

Like so many of those serving their country, Jason was the embodiment of patriotism and honor. The horrific attack on our country on September 11, 2001 cast his future and he left for Parris Island just three days after graduation from high school at only seventeen years of age. He believed, as you do, that this is a war of necessity and absolutely needs to be addressed on their soil, not ours.

Jason went to Iraq with the ideal of defending our freedoms even though many of his fellow countrymen exercised theirs by condemning what he did. Once there, he immediately grasped the importance of being part of the vast effort to liberate the Iraqi people and bring them a semblance of the democracy we enjoy. This filled him with as much purpose and importance as what he had originally viewed as his mission to keep terrorism from the doorstep of his brothers.

Jason lived only long enough to know that the elections were deemed a success and to feel the relief that the numbers of voters were greater than anticipated and the number of casualties far less. He had many concerns that the battles waged and the lives given may not be enough to insure the liberation that we have all prayed for. He knew that the final verdict of success would rest as a tally in a record of history. He knew for the meantime, however, that to fight the battle against tyranny and to march ahead under the banner of freedom was work that God himself had commissioned.

While I was lost in my grief and struggling to continue forth with the mundane details that these times require of the surviving loved ones, I heard your voice call to me. You had come into my living room and were standing among my family. You were delivering The State of the Union Address, but that was only the venue you used to chat with me. You reminded me of the pride of country and love of life that filled my son. I was able to look into the eyes of the man he so deeply respected and I knew exactly why he was so proud to deploy and fight on your orders. I knew, as he did that the loss of but one life was too many and that your decision was not one that you made without the heavy weight of human cost.

You steadied my trembling being and cradled my breaking heart delicately in your mighty hands. You lifted my chin and my gaze was held by someone who felt the loss of our troops and the grief of their families. You implored us, even without words, not to break ranks but to continue to hold strong our bond of determination to end terrorism so our children, and their children, may someday sleep in peace throughout the world.

You brought with you friends. I swelled with pride at the young Iraqi woman who was born into a life of oppression as were those born before her. She told me that on Monday, she opened her eyes to see the faint light of hope for the first time in her life. She showed me her fingers that were stained with the blood of my son. That vote reminds us all that my child did not die in vain!

You also introduced me to another family who, like us, had let go of their son's hand to send him away to pay the ultimate price for our beliefs. Their tears mingled with mine and their warmth filled my very soul. Their pride, their anguish, was mine and ultimately, their unwavering support of their President shone like mine all around us.

When that chamber filled with people erupting in applause time and time again, I felt a peace engulf me that has sustained me throughout the days since.

We laid my son, America's son, to rest in Arlington National Cemetery yesterday and committed him to a piece of hallowed ground reserved for the celebration of the values and beliefs that the rest of us could only aspire to hold so dearly. He shared your vision, honored your courage, and proudly fought on your command. He also prayed every night that God would grant you the strength and wisdom to make the decisions that only you can make.

We share your vision, honor your courage and offer the same prayers for you, your family and all those who advise you. You reminded me of all of those things during your visit to my home. It is with that great gift that I humbly say thank you and may God Bless the United States of America.

Sincerely,
Rhonda L. Winfield
97 Twin Springs Lane
Stuarts Draft, VA 24477

I felt as if something significant in my path to healing had just transpired and for a brief moment it seemed as if maybe someday my world would be livable again.

I received a kind and lovely reply from the President several weeks later. I had never really expected one. I hear he is rather busy, after all. I had already been sent a letter of sympathy, which he had actually signed and I had framed and hung in Jason's room. This new letter was accompanied by a presidential coin. I will cherish it for all my days as a reminder that even, but for a few moments, the leader of the free world heard my heart and shared in my grief.

The next few weeks were a virtual blur. Justin remained at home and we somehow drew something from each other that managed to sustain us both. Outside of our walls, out in the real world, that comfort didn't exist, so we had to stay in the safety of our home together. We just somehow helped to pull each other along. Neither of us wanted to talk about our pain or loss because we wanted to protect the other. It is still that way.

I hated in some ways that Justin was too big to hold on my lap and comfort like I could Courtland and Carter. He was so proud and strong and had such difficulty letting people into the tender inner zone. He didn't know what to do to help and heal his mother. My role had always been that of "fixer." What are you supposed to do when the fixer is broken?

The fact that his father and I were divorced made many situations difficult. This was not the time that any of us needed to try to decide the decorum of certain seating arrangements, or positioning in receiving lines, or any of the things that would be an issue when the family "unit" was not a neat little grouping reminiscent of *Leave it to Beaver.*

Justin seemed so lost. He was the older brother. He was the one who should have been there, in his mind. He was the one who was used to leading and now was left to follow something that he could not see. He had become the invisible sibling. The stories were all of a hero's life and legacy and of the little brothers that were left behind. Justin was just someone in the fray. I talked about him proudly in every interview but because he chose not to be in front of the cameras, or to speak out publicly, he was simply excess information. He was left in the shadow of something that was undefined and haunting and he had no idea where to go to find the light.

We all plowed through the "thank you" notes and endless matters that seem to come from such life events. So many details. So much time lost. We were busy for what seemed like every minute of the day and yet we could not tell you what we had accomplished and seemed to be marking very little off of our "to do" list. We just kept hoping each night when we went to bed that tomorrow would be the day that we would get back into the game of life. Tomorrow this would all be behind us and we would embark on our journey to our new normalcy-whatever that would be. Tomorrow, however, never seemed to dawn.

Courtland and Carter had been home-schooled up to this point and I kept believing that the next day would gift me with the ability to focus and begin schooling again. It never came. I would eventually enroll them in a private school where they had attended a part-time summer program and had wonderful teachers helping them to prepare for the coming school year. They love everything about the school and we are so thankful for Mr. Spencer and everyone at Good Shepherd for the way they accepted our broken little family and built us all up with their love.

Justin and Missy returned to West Virginia after several weeks and tried to re-engage in their lives. While I know he felt a million miles from home sometimes, this was also the very thing that insulated him from getting held down in the grief here at home. He had the ability to run away just far enough to be on the periphery of his brother's death. This may, in fact, be what saved him.

I had tried to return to work but found myself unable. I was under a lot of pressure at the time to return or possibly lose my job. I knew that without a college education, I would have great difficulty finding another job that paid as well and offered equal benefits. I would certainly not find such a job that required me to only work daylight hours and be home on weekends with my family. I had to somehow make it work.

I cried all day long at first. Then, it improved to just sitting by the road crying in spells. I considered this a great improvement and a positive sign that things could get better. I fought with everything I had, came home and cried every night and just prayed to God to give me the strength to take another run at it the next day. That carried me through until the day I received the phone call.

I was on the last section of my route, which is one of the very few places that I have cell phone service. The call came and I pulled over to answer it. Courtland was on the line and was very upset.

"They came," he said. "They came." His voice was low and he was obviously holding back tears. "What came?" I inquired. "The boxes," he said sadly.

I knew immediately what he meant. Jason's personal affects had arrived from Iraq.

★ My favorite picture of Jason. He is four years old.

★ Jason, the day Scott and I married, June 8, 1991.

★ Giddy Up! Jason believed everyone should learn to be at one with a horse.

★ Father J. Kevin Fox

★ A cowboy and a gentleman. This photo was taken in 1998. Jason was almost 13 years old.

★ Our family portrait, 1999.

★ Cowboys, brothers and friends.

Above Left: ★ Jason and I at my sister's wedding. **Above Right:** ★ Even school photos were rarely taken without his cowboy hat. (2002)

"Cowards die many times before their death; the valiant never taste of death but once." -- William Shakespeare

"It is not what you take with you when you leave this world, but what you leave behind you when you go."

Jason Redifer
Stuarts Draft, Virginia

"I'm here for a good time, not a long time."

"Ask not what your country can do for you; ask what you can do for your country." - John F. Kennedy

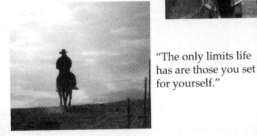

"The only limits life has are those you set for yourself."

"Let us endeavor so to live that when we come to die even the undertaker will be sorry." -Mark Twain

"We have nothing to fear but fear itself" - FDR

"Live, laugh, love." - Clay Walker

"God bless the U.S.A." U.S.M.C. "Semper Fi!"

★ The page in Jason's senior yearbook that tells of a haunting wisdom.

★ Jason's senior portrait, December 2002.

★ Jason and his best friend, Amanda Mc-Connell, at their graduation form Stuart Hall in May 2003. Jason left for Parris Island three days later at age 17.

★ Boot camp graduation at Parris Island, South Carolina on August 29, 2003.

★ Jason's official U.S. Marine portrait.

★ This photograph was taken by Julie Dodd, a professional photographer, just before Jason's deployment. She titled it "Joy Ride." Julie commented on the experience: "I was blessed and honored that my life was touched by Jason, if only for a moment; a gentleman with a true cowboy spirit."

★ Jason proudly standing in front of his newly purchased car just before his deployment. (May, 2004)

★ This was the last photo taken of Justin and Jason. This was at our picnic, the evening before Jason left for good. (June 12, 2004)

★ This was my Christmas gift in 2004. Jason knew he would be in Iraq during Christmas so he talked his brother into having it made before he left.

★ One of the few smiles we saw from Iraq. This photo came home in a disposable camera in his effects.

★ This picture from Iraq defines Jason, both in spirit and deed.

★ One of the fifteen photos retrieved from Jason's broken digital camera.

★ "When presented the flag at Jason's burial, I was moved to reach out to the empathetic Marine who touched my heart with his kind eyes."

Photograph by Mike Tripp, courtesy of the News Leader.

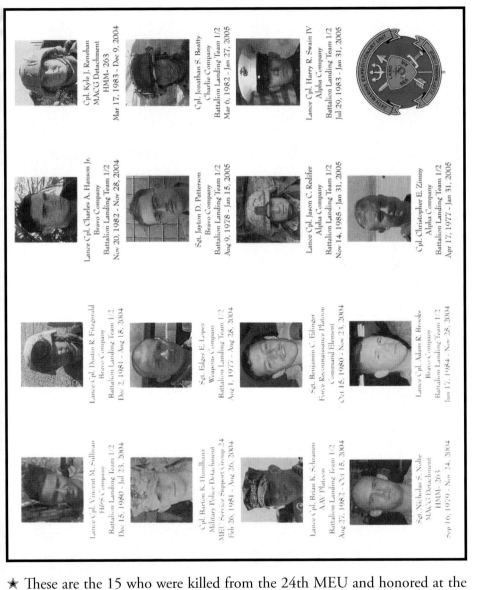

Cpl. Kyle J. Renehan
MACG Detachment
HMM-263
Mar 17, 1983 - Dec 9, 2004

Cpl. Jonathan S. Beatty
Charlie Company
Battalion Landing Team 1/2
Mar 6, 1982 - Jan 27, 2005

Lance Cpl. Harry R. Swain IV
Alpha Company
Battalion Landing Team 1/2
Jul 29, 1983 - Jan 31, 2005

Lance Cpl. Charles A. Hanson Jr.
Bravo Company
Battalion Landing Team 1/2
Nov 20, 1982 - Nov 28, 2004

Sgt. Jayton D. Patterson
Bravo Company
Battalion Landing Team 1/2
Aug 9, 1978 - Jan 15, 2005

Lance Cpl. Jason C. Redifer
Alpha Company
Battalion Landing Team 1/2
Nov 14, 1985 - Jan 31, 2005

Cpl. Christopher E. Zimny
Alpha Company
Battalion Landing Team 1/2
Apr 17, 1977 - Jan 31, 2005

Lance Cpl. Dustin R. Fitzgerald
Bravo Company
Battalion Landing Team 1/2
Dec 2, 1981 - Aug 18, 2004

Sgt. Edgar E. Lopez
Weapons Company
Battalion Landing Team 1/2
Aug 1, 1977 - Aug 28, 2004

Sgt. Benjamin C. Edinger
Force Reconnaissance Platoon
Command Element
Oct 15, 1980 - Nov 23, 2004

Lance Cpl. Adam R. Brooks
Bravo Company
Battalion Landing Team 1/2
Jun 17, 1984 - Nov 28, 2004

Lance Cpl. Vincent M. Sullivan
H&S Company
Battalion Landing Team 1/2
Dec 15, 1980 - Jul 23, 2004

Cpl. Barton R. Humlhanz
Military Police Detachment
MEU Service Support Team 24
Feb 26, 1981 - Aug 26, 2004

Lance Cpl. Brian K. Schramm
AAV Platoon
Battalion Landing Team 1/2
Aug 27, 1982 - Oct 15, 2004

Sgt. Nicholas S. Nolte
MACG Detachment
HMM-263
Sep 16, 1979 - Nov 24, 2004

★ These are the 15 who were killed from the 24th MEU and honored at the memorial service at Camp Lejeune on March 31, 2005.

★ This was the last photo taken of the last mission of Jason in Iraq.

★ This picture was taken on what would have been Jason's 20th birthday and our first one at Arlington. (November 14, 2005)

CHAPTER 7

THE FINAL JOURNEY HOME

When I walked in the door they were the first things I saw. Two large boxes stared at me and dared me to come closer. Courtland and Carter were standing over them as though they were keeping some sort of vigil. These boxes were something sacred. Inside would be all that we would ever have back from Jason.

The boys looked at me for deliverance. They waited to receive something from me that would tell them what to expect and to give them comfort from their fears. I had neither. I called Scott on his cell phone to tell him that I was home and that I was going to open the boxes. He was on his way. I circled around the boxes like a vulture waiting to smell weakness. I observed them from every angle. They were dirty and squashed and from the outside didn't seem threatening at all. I could read that the return address was from Camp LeJeune. I decided that the contents must have been sent there first and then forwarded to me.

I told the boys that it would never be any easier so we were just going to sit down right there on the floor and open them. We would go through the contents and see just what kind of a story these boxes had to tell us.

I remember shaking all over as I cut through the tape on the first one. As soon as the flap was lifted the smell of sweat wafted over me. I knew that it was the smell of the desert, the smell of combat, the smell of death. It was sweet, yet it was pungent. It was primal and it filled the air. As I began to pull things out, I was able to see Jason in every item I touched. A heavy blanket consumed most of one box. I could see the warrior that was LCPL Redifer huddled in this soft covering. I saw him trying to find warmth while he battled the visions that only came when he allowed himself to close his eyes. It was as if these things were talking to me. There was a narrative beginning and illustrated visions came crisply into my mind with each and every word being spoken to me by the spirit dwelling within these cardboard confines. I saw in that blanket the cold of the darkness but more importantly the only warmth that would insulate him from the reality of what he had done before his rest.

I pulled out a pair of worn out flip-flops. They were imprinted by his feet and the bottoms were worn smooth from continued usage in the sand. I saw him scamper back and forth, in his most vulnerable state, heading to and from the showers. I wanted to laugh at this vision and it seemed so strange to me that someone responsible for assembling these things would have chosen to include these shoes. I was surprised that this item had not been discarded. I don't know why they made the grade but I felt fortunate to have them. They are dear to me and rest in his closet to this day. Periodically, I will pick them up just to watch a few grains of sand fall off. That sand is somehow holy to me.

There were many pieces of equipment included that had not been part of his standard register. Those items he had been issued by the Marines had been sorted out and returned to stock. I am quite sure when new recruits are being issued gas masks that they never once consider the previous possessor. I'm certain it is just thought of as one more thing that has come from an endless supply of military surplus and not an item, removed from a backpack, before the final disposition of belongings to a next of kin.

I put the goggles that I removed on my head and I saw the desert, the sand, the heat, and the mission. I saw freedom just beyond what I could focus on. I took them off and placed them aside.

I pulled out something from deep in one of the corners. I pulled up his dog tags. They were the ones that he had been issued originally at Parris Island. I lost my vision temporarily to the overflow of tears. I held them close to my heart and felt it breaking once again. I could not even try to hold it back for the children's sake. This was all we got. This was the ugly reality. No stellar performances or optimistic outlook would bend this into anything but the horrible truth. Our family had paid the highest price for freedom and we were just now getting the receipt. I put them around my neck and they remain there to this day. They always will. I thought about why we had been unable to receive the set he had been wearing and I felt sick.

I looked up to see Scott standing in the doorway, close enough to witness yet far enough to keep himself removed from the vacuum of intolerable loss that was sucking me in. Denial is easiest, after all, from a distance. What words could he offer now? What could he do but watch me lose myself somewhere in my imagination as I poured over these little pieces of our son's last months on this Earth.

Courtland and Carter each handled the items as I discarded them. They sat with patience and allowed me to venture in first, seemingly knowing what I needed from the journey. They would take turns fondling every crevice and surface of every item and I realized the movie had begun to play for them as well.

The second box was filled with smaller items like a compact disc player that my friend, Tammy, had sent him for his birthday. Tammy was another friend that had met my sons during the first few years of their lives and had helped love them into adulthood.

I knew when she tried to be upbeat about sending Jason's birthday package that she was hurting as well over the fact that he would be turning nineteen years old in a place so far from home. I worried that the CD player would get sand in it and not work for very long but I quickly deduced that it wouldn't matter. Surely, Tammy Estes had reasoned this as well and it was now obvious that it was about the giving of love from home, not the longevity of electronics. She also sent his favorite music and all of the snacks and treats from home that he would have missed.

When I held this CD player in my hands, I saw his joy in receiving it. I saw him playing his discs and shutting out the vulgar truth that was his world there. I knew what I was holding represented a sweet piece of family to Jason.

I found the digital camera that I had given him right before he left. I told him that since he was going to be gone for his birthday and Christmas that he might as well have some gift to open before he left. I really could not afford to buy it at the time that I did, but I knew that Jason would only have one opportunity to see all that was ahead of him. Life doesn't always wait until good decisions are easy. As it turned out, that camera was the best investment that I had ever made.

The camera, not the CD player, had ceased working due to sand. The memory card inside, however, was undamaged and from that card we were able to retrieve about fifteen photos. Those pictures are priceless to me. They are all of Jason. I found this very bazaar that it was always others who had his camera and that they were shooting him. What an extraordinary blessing. Of course, during the time on my living room floor, I only knew that the camera had potential to bring us closer to Jason's world.

The little index cards from his going away picnic were the next item to be removed. They were worn and smeared a little and kept together by a rubber band. They had obviously been used as we had intended. I slipped them out of the band and read them all again. I read them out loud to us all and we sat in silence for a while as their power washed over us.

The stuffed donkey that was one of the characters from the movie, "Shrek," came out of the box next. This brought a round of laughter from us all and I felt a sort of salve for our souls. That donkey had logged quite a few miles and was responsible for quite a few laughs at times when humor was hard to find.

There was another tiny object shining in a corner and when I pulled it out, I almost discarded it. It was a bottle cap. Upon further inspection, I realized it was a SoBe bottle cap and on the underside it read: BE A HERO.

Courtland looked over my shoulder and read the bottle cap out loud. "Well, I guess he did just that," he said so reassuringly. He then went on to explain what he meant to Carter who seemed to find great pride and comfort in the thought.

I picked a label off of the bottom. It was an address for my friend, Roxanne. She had sent him a package and he must have cut the return address off so he could send her a thank you card. I guess the fact that it came home with most of the personal items he held dear there would have to be enough now.

The last items in the box were the sacred cowboy boots. They were still rolled up, still a part of Jason. These hurt the most to retrieve. It was wrong to have the boots and not the cowboy.

After sorting through the other odds and ends that were left we carefully folded everything back up and returned all but the dog tags and the SoBe cap to the box. The cap remains on a shelf in Jason's room. This small reminder with a mighty message sits in wait for when we need to remember what he believed in and how he lived his short life.

We left the boxes in the middle of the floor where we had been going through them. They remained there until the following weekend when Justin came home. Together, we sorted through them. He started making a little stack of some of the things that he wanted to keep with him. He was already somehow wearing the boots. These would be the most important to him. They were the ruby slippers that, while lacking the power to bring Jason back home, would serve as a reminder of why he went searching for Oz in the first place.

Another item from the box caught Justin's attention. It was a key ring I had made for Jason after he left and sent it as a reminder of home and all that he was fighting for. I had laminated different pictures and then strung them together on a clip that he could fasten to a backpack or similar item. There were special photos of all of his family members. One of the President and First Lady another of the Twin Towers that Jason had taken himself. One of Jason on the porch swing with Courtland and Carter in his lap and one of the last photos ever made of him and Justin, etc. It was emptiness, exponentially so.

The following day I went to the mailbox for yet another surprise. Jason had not finished speaking to me after all. In the mail was a large envelope from Aberdeen Proving Ground, Maryland.

The contents still intrigue me. I had assumed that these contents would have been what were retrieved from Jason's body but under the circumstances of the accident, I couldn't see how this was possible. The envelope held a few personal items, a page from a book and a detailed inventory of the items enclosed that had been signed off on by someone from the Joint Personal Effects Depot.

The contents were listed as:
1 Holder, coin, brown in color
1 Multi-tool, mini, inscribed Chapter Sixteen 119/120
1 Drivers license, Virginia, inscribed Redifer, Jason Charles
3 Cards, phone, 2-inscribed MCI, 670 minutes, 1-inscribed AT&T, 550 units
1 Card, training, SWET Training Facility
1 Card, inscribed VISA, Marine Federal Credit Union, Jason D. Redifer
1 Card, inscribed VISA, FSNB, Jason C. Redifer

I held every item as though by touching it would help me to feel a little bit of him. Although thoroughly confused by the contents, the page from the book stumped me the most. I could never see how this item could have survived the accident and have never had an explanation as to where these items were recovered. The message it delivered was directly from beyond the grave. I believe that Jason had saved this page because the vivid description of the sandstorm was something that he understood and wanted to share with us. He was an avid reader of Louis L'Amour and other western novels and shared those with his fellow Marines, as well. This page was from a novel titled *"Last Stand at Papago*

Wells" and comes from pages 119 and 120. The portion he had marked read:

"*There is upon the great sand wastes no more terrible thing than a sand storm...the driving grains of sand wipe out the earth and sky, obscure the horizons, and close one in a tight and lonely world no more than a few feet square. Until one has experienced a sand storm upon the desert one cannot know horror; until one has felt the lashing whips of sand one cannot know agony; and until one has felt that heat, that terror, that feeling that all the world has gone wrong, one has not known hell.*"

"*The birds cease to fly, the tiny animals, even the insects hunt their hidden places. Horses roll their eyes, wild with terror, and men find places to hide from the stifling dust. Yet it is not the wind, not the sand, nor the heat alone, it is the terror, the frantic choking, the gasping, the struggle and the cowering fear brought on in part by the quivering electricity in the air, the unbearable tension, the loss of all perspective. Our senses are fragile things, dainty things, occasionally trustworthy, yet always demanding of perspective. Our senses need horizons, they need gauges, the need rules by which to apply themselves, and in the sandstorm there is no horizon and there are no rules. There is no near or far, any high or low, no cold or warm, there is only that moving wall of wind that roars out of distance, screaming insanely, screaming and roaring. And with it the uncounted trillions of lashing sand bits. One moves at the bottom of a moving sea, a literal sea of sand, whose surface is somewhere high above in the great vault of the heavens, and one dies choking, crawling on the hands and knees, choking with sand, choking with wind, choking with the effort to breathe.*"

"Such a storm was coming now."

The book page had arrived in a Ziploc type bag. When I gently removed it I was surprised at how fragile it was. It was smooth and the front and back of the page were becoming one. It had obviously been handled a lot.

After reading the passage, I carefully returned it to the plastic bag where it is still today.

I have thought of that passage many times. Those powerful words, that incredible description had struck a chord of truth and understanding with Jason. He read in those words a kinship to a man who had lived a part of the life he was experiencing. He read in those words what he wanted us to know about a segment of his time there. He read in those words a message that he would carry with him until it could become a letter from beyond.

I put the other items in his desk drawer where he would have placed them if he had made it home. I open the drawer and just finger through them from time to time. It is closeness that I seek when I run my fingers over their surfaces to feel something that may have touched his skin.

I wrap myself in his blanket some days and sit in his chair and read his magical page. I see him there. I feel the sting of the sand pelting his face. I watch him grimace and squeeze tightly his eyes. I feel his fear. It is all something that is alive, at least.

There were many things that I had hoped would return home but did not. I had always hoped that the letters from home that he treasured might someday find their way back. I had also always hoped for a letter that Jason might have written to us just in case. I know everything that he ever had to say had already been said a million times and yet I longed for it once more.

There would never be enough. No matter what we would have received, we would have always wanted a little more. There is nothing that can fill the void. No stack of letters, no final words in life, no pieces of a story...nothing would have made this chapter complete for us. We would always be missing a very significant portion for which we craved. Jason would not be coming home. No amount of remnants would ease that. Yet, every single piece was a treasure unto itself. Each item, no matter how insignificant was essential. Yet another contradiction that had become my life. It was all too much. It was not nearly enough.

CHAPTER 8

CAMP LEJEUNE MEMORIAL SERVICE

The invitation was for March 31st, 2005 at 3:00pm. Our presence was being requested by the Commanding Officer of the 24th Marine Expeditionary Unit, II Expeditionary Force for a memorial service at W.P.T. Hill Field, Camp LeJeune, North Carolina. This was to be a service honoring the fifteen young men who lost their lives while serving with the 24th MEU during this last tour in Iraq.

I had such mixed feelings as we headed south. I was anxious to be around all those that had known Jason and to have an opportunity for us all to experience a farewell service together. These men had been afforded no opportunity to attend the funerals of their comrades. Their horror and grief in the field had to be checked and put on hold to enable them to keep their focus and strength. The danger for them was not over until they were safely home. They were reminded of this all too quickly when the attack on January 31st occurred.

I was relieved to know that I would be meeting the families of the two other Marines who lost their lives alongside my son that day. I had spoken briefly on the phone to one father and was secretly expecting some sort of healing to fall down upon us as we gathered together in both pride and grief. Safety in numbers. I would discover that it was more of the blind leading the blind. We were all so very different and grieved in as many different ways. We were all at various places in our grief and we all had very different expectations of what we would take away from Camp LeJeune that weekend. Like our Marines, themselves, all unique, yet all of one.

We would call one another several times in the coming year and some of us would correspond occasionally. I know they were all in my heart every day that passed and I felt very connected to each of them as we all faced shared time markers such as the anniversary of our sons' deaths. Yet, to speak over the phone at such times and to hear a reflection of the pain in my own heart was almost too much to bear. I think so much of my coping came from 'good ol' denial and having to interact with someone who would strip that away and take me straight to the very place that I could not allow myself to go was direct suicide for me. A polite gesture such as a card that reminded them that they were in my prayers would have to suffice. I would open the kind and generous offerings from the Zimny family that would seem to find me every time I needed a little empathy and understanding. Their brief words were always loving, kind and uplifting yet dripped of pain from a collective heart that seemingly would never repair itself. I would hold each envelope while warm, salty tears would stream down my face and both the gift extended and the need left wanting from this family engulfed me. There was simply too much pain in one another's presence and yet we were the only source of understanding for each other.

I think that somehow just being able to finally make the trip to Camp Lejuene was a temporary reprieve for me. I had been so lost when I didn't get to go for the long-awaited homecoming. Finally, I was in the car headed to the destination that had been waiting for me. I know now that somehow I believed it would all turn back the clock. I was running as fast as I could go toward a brick wall. I never saw it coming.

There was a sense of excitement as we entered the gates of the base. I could never help but feel a part of something so special as we lost ourselves in one of these military cities. This was a different world. This was a world of the protectors and conquerors. This was the sacred place that existed to keep the outside world safe.

Through my oldest sons, we were a part of this great unknown to civilians, and pride consumed me. I entered the registration office to sign us in and get directions for where we were to be going. I announced myself and my reason for visiting and was met with what I deemed to be the appropriate courtesy of such. Once we were through the main gate and past the guardhouse it all started to settle in.

I felt a little off balance. My breath was a little short and my head a little fuzzy. Buildings and fields passed that I had become familiar with and suddenly the gravity of the fact hit me. Jason was not here. There was nothing in this vast military metropolis that was Jason anymore. He would never again tour us around. We would never try to find his dorm. We would never watch him drill again. Jason was dead and we were here to acknowledge that. I was suddenly back in my living room with the CACO officers signing papers. My son was dead. There would be no viewable body. He was in pieces. They would be sending home what they could find. They would not disturb my insanity to let me know if further pieces were to be retrieved in the future. The funeral expenses would be covered. I could choose a wood or metal casket. There would be a Marine guard with his remains at all times. "I'm sorry Ma'am." "We'll take our leave now."

I was almost gasping for air by now. I can remember hearing Scott's voice as though he was in a tunnel. His words were warped and muffled but I could tell he was annoyed by something. We arrived at the area where we were required to check in and assemble our group, which consisted of several vehicles. Scott was mumbling about our little caravan of cars not staying together during the drive down and I wondered why he really cared. I suspected he was really bothered by something else and assumed that the whole base experience was negatively affecting him as well.

While waiting, I began to think about Justin who was coming down later with his father. I was starting to feel angry that he hadn't chosen to come with me. I had tried not to be defensive of his time with his dad during this entire ordeal but there were many times when it was difficult to share him.

I began recalling my horror when the CACO officers informed me that my ex-husband would be technically the next of kin due to his age. I was told that without regard to whomever is designated as the next of kin by the deceased, the older parent would be the official next of kin for purposes of the United States Marine Corps. Talk about a knife in the heart. I was standing in my home, trying to remain upright after hearing of my son's death and the salt in the wound was that Jason's biological father would be making the decisions regarding funeral arrangements, burial, disposition of personal property, etc., as far as the involvement of the U.S. Marine Corps. I was even told that the burial flag would be presented to him.

I can tell you that as a mother, I knew as soon as I had heard the words, that NO ONE would be leaving that cemetery with MY burial flag. If they had to pry me off that casket as I was beating back someone with my high heel shoe, then so be it. I was Jason's mother. I would have his burial flag. I brought my son into this world and I would be holding the symbol of his life when he was laid to rest. Period.

As it ended up, a separate flag had been folded and was displayed beside Jason's casket at the church. Apparently, we were not the first divorced parents of a deceased Marine in the history of the Armed Services. Although we both received citations and Purple Heart accommodations for Jason, the actual presentation at the church delivered the Purple Heart and the folded flag to his father. I was then presented the burial flag at Arlington. Much to my relief and great comfort, all decisions were made in accordance with my wishes. We both tried very hard to bridge the vast differences in our lives and be respectful of one another. We didn't even vaguely know one another any more but we remembered who we once had been to each other and we tried to form a new relationship based on that and our shared loss. Justin had often been lost in the middle. There were times now when I reached out for him and he was holding up his father. I felt that he was exactly where he should be, yet I longed to be by his side. They were leaning on each other, isolated from everything else in a way that only they would understand and yet it was one more thing that I had to accept.

I believe it was my jealously over that shared isolation that made me so annoyed at the moment, back at Camp Lejeune. I was simply jealous that Justin wasn't with me. Then, I became angry with myself because I knew how selfish and ridiculous that was.

As I tried to clear my mind of the fog that had sat in, I began to realize that the barely audible sounds that Scott had been making were now turning into recognizable, unavoidable, anger. He had become frustrated and annoyed as well and we were both on the edge of a fit when the others all arrived for check in. We were suddenly like children that could not be left alone! We had both, in very different ways, found ourselves on the verge of a tantrum! Sadly, neither of us had a clue to what we were really so angry about.

When everyone in our party had been eventually assigned a room we began the task of settling in. As Scott and I began ferrying luggage to and from the parking lot, we began to quarrel over who was or was not carrying enough! We were needing to vent these horrible feelings and were lacking the skills to do it productively.

The argument quickly escalated and resulted in me standing by the car crying desperately. Here I was in this place that in my mind's eye was to have been a sanctuary for my shattered resolve and everything was crumbling faster than I could scurry to pick it back up. I had almost lost consciousness just driving into the facility. I had a minor fit with myself over who did or did not ride with me. I became completely overwhelmed by the thought of a former husband who was obviously orchestrating a plot to steal away my eldest son, had suffered a near stroke over a relatively simple hotel check in process and was now having a meltdown in the parking lot. I had just decided that my current husband was clearly an ass not to understand all of this and that the whole world was poised to damn me. When somehow despite these evil forces, I sucked it up, entered the building we were assigned to and banged my pull along up two flights of stairs.

Once inside the room, I began to pontificate about the unjust state of things as I flung clothing all around me. Scott was just looking out the window, refusing to further engage me. When my frustration of not being acknowledged was about to bubble over, he turned to look at me. Huge tears fell from his eyes and he looked as if he had just been destroyed. I stopped mid rant and went to him. He just looked down at me as though I had never babbled a stupid whining word and said, "I just can't do this. He isn't here and I don't want to be here either. I have to go home."

I was shocked. I had somehow loaded him up on the "Denial Express" and he had ridden that train in with me. Now our ugly reality consumed us both as we rode it right into the concrete barrier at the end of the tunnel. We had been expecting the light of day to deliver us into the other side and instead we slammed into the darkness and now, picking himself up, he just wanted to run home.

You know your situation is dire when someone who normally pulls you together with their reserved and calm nature has just checked out. I had a total "we are so screwed" moment and then somehow I just reached for my husband. We fell into each other's arms and sobbed. We sobbed for our lost son, we sobbed for the brother that our boys would never grow up knowing. Mostly, we just sobbed because we had landed somewhere that we were afraid we would never be delivered from, a place in the abyss where light is an unknown concept.

When the tears subsided and we caught our breath we lay across the bed and made a game plan. We could leave and return home but we wouldn't. We didn't know if we could make it through but we were going to stay and try to take everything away from this experience that we could. This was Jason's goodbye to Camp LeJeune and we were going to make it ours as well.

We called the room next door and told my mother, my sister-in-law and the boys to get ready to go to dinner. A little time together to relax and get some food in our empty stomachs would help us all to get some perspective and prepare for the events that were to begin the following morning.

My sister-in-law, Avis, was taking good care of my mother. I was so thankful because I had absolutely nothing to offer my mom. I knew she was completely devastated and while I usually tried my best to make sure she was well taken care of when she needed it, I could barely even talk to her now. We had driven to her house after the Marines had delivered that horrible news to us to pick her up before she heard it from anyone else. I just walked in her door, started crying and told her Jason had been killed. She went into panic mode as well and quickly gathered her things to come with me at my request. She busied herself literally all through the night doing dishes, laundry and anything else that she could think of. She would not let herself stop and have this tragedy catch up to her. My mother had survived a difficult life by learning early on how to take control and to disassociate. She was exceptional now.

A full year later, I have still been unable to really address the loss of my son with my mother. I cannot watch this woman who has never relinquished her authority to anything falter with grief. Likewise, I know she is suffering not just for herself but in having to watch her child grieve. We know the other is there. I guess that will have to be enough for now.

I had always been blessed to be surrounded by strong women in my life. I'll never forget seeing Avis come into my house that awful January evening. She rolled in, seized control of a crisis and started handling details. She basically dressed me, fed me (or at least kept shoving food in my direction and threatening me) and led me in whatever direction I needed to go at any given time. Months later I was still calling her and asking her to handle things that as my "personal assistant and secretary" she should take care of. The first time I tried to have a "normal" evening with Courtland and Carter (also the first time Scott left me at home alone for a while to go play basketball) I ended up calling Avis to see if she could come over. I had promised to take the boys for pizza at a nearby store and suddenly found myself paralyzed with the fear of leaving the house alone. She came over, picked us all up and took us to the pizza parlor. She had eaten already but sat with us while we pretended to be normal. I don't know how I would have managed without her. She was not someone I even really knew all that well before this. We were related by marriage and certainly liked one another but never really had spent time together. That has certainly changed. I will never forget what she did for me and my family and I will owe her forever for it. She had known Jason well and loved him dearly and in taking care of me she did the one thing for him that he would have asked for.

My girlfriend Tammy and her family would also come to Camp LeJeune. She had been helping to hold Justin together and waited patiently, as I believe she still does, ready to jump up and do the "it" that will comfort me and help me heal. She is the one who just leaves the "I'm here" message on the phone when she knows I won't pick it up. She's the one who just shows up with "monster cookies" that I believe have magical healing powers on days when she knows tears will be blinding me. She's the one who sees beyond anything I try to put out there and let's me think I'm fooling her. Of course, she would be there for the service.

Others came from out of town as well. Two of Jason's special friends from Stuart Hall had come. Lauren Chadwick had taken Jason to her home in North Carolina over a break and he had become an unofficial member of her family. The Chadwick Clan showed up in full support.

Jason's friend Amanda also came with her father. She made the journey from Michigan. Jason and Amanda had met their freshman year at Stuart Hall and neither had been in a private school before. They instantly bonded and eventually went on to have a kind of relationship that few of us are ever privileged to know in this lifetime. Most marriages I know of never have the honesty and devotion that these two shared. They never dated, however, because they never could. They had something so beyond the boyfriend/girlfriend realm that they really didn't know what to do with it but they certainly were not about to gamble it away by dating! Jason made Amanda promise to look after me and true to

92

her word she has called me every week without fail. She is so much more than just Jason's faithful friend. She is my friend. Our relationship started because of Jason but is no longer defined by him.

We knew all of these friends would be there for us the following day and as we went to bed that night, we talked about how uplifted we were by their support. We knew they were coming for Jason. We knew they were coming for us.

Tomorrow, we would honor the fallen. Tomorrow, we would bid them farewell. Tomorrow, we would commit them to our memories. Tomorrow, another piece of me would die but what would remain would be held tightly in the fold of those who loved us.

CHAPTER 9

STILL IN THE EUPHORIA

It was a beautiful, sun filled morning when we awakened in North Carolina. The air was still a little crisp but not surprising for March. There were several details I needed to take care of on base before we were to report for a luncheon scheduled with the commanding officers.

I had planned on donating Jason's dress blue uniform to Stuart Hall and needed to have his insignia upgraded. He had been promoted to the rank of Lance Corporal while in Iraq and his uniform needed to reflect this.

I was sent to the Marine Corps Exchange on base only to find that the store had not yet opened for the day and would not until long after I would need to leave. The captain who was assisting me tried to contact someone within the store to speak to them but everyone was busy helping a young Marine get fitted for a uniform. We were soon to discover that this Marine was Jamel.

He had been transferred from Bethesda Naval Medical Center in Maryland to Walter Reed Army Hospital in Washington D.C. for continued care and physical therapy. The commanding officer for the 24th MEU, Colonel Johnson, had arranged to have him brought to Camp Lejeune for the Memorial Service. This would be the first time he would be back at base since the unit's deployment to Iraq. He was in the process of being fitted for the uniform of the day. When I found out he was there, I insisted on being allowed to see him. The captain with me sent word and I soon saw Jamel being wheeled over to the door. We fell into each other's arms and held on for comfort and restoration. After a brief visit he was returned to finish his fitting and we were introduced to Master Sergeant Glenn Wilson, USMC (Retired). He was the manager of the Military Clothing Sales and Service and was opening the store just for us. He extended his deepest sympathy and once again I was facing another

Marine who pained for the loss of one of their own. Mr. Wilson had lived long enough to see many other Marines pass and yet obviously the emotion was far from routine and stale. He was genuinely hurting for us and with us. I gave him the uniform and he busied himself gathering all that I would need. He then took me to the alterations department and introduced me to Jean Forte, who was head of that department. I could tell immediately that they had worked together for a long time and had a very respectful rapport. They could communicate almost without words. She knew instinctively what he was wanting, what he expected and he knew he could count on her to accomplish exactly that with professionalism and integrity. I was unable to say much to either of them by this point. I was again becoming overwhelmed with emotion from the intensity of it all. My mother and Avis handled the details that required input or information from us. Scott had stayed outside with Courtland and Carter.

I was treated like a queen in that Exchange that day and I found a friend that I would never forget. While waiting for the uniform to be pressed, Jean came from around the counter to speak directly with me. She told me, with tears welling in her eyes, of her sympathies for our family as well as her pride in my son as a Marine. She told me that she too was a Marine and that she and Mr. Wilson were the only two employees in the store that were. She felt they were taking this personally because even though neither knew Jason, he was one of them. She was very visibly moved and her words and sentiment resonated in me in a way that affected me deeply.

A beautiful job was done on the uniform. They had worked for Jason. I would never forget their pride in their country, their love of mankind, their commitment to the Corps and their devotion to the families of the fallen. These two were Semper Fi.

I would correspond with Jean quite a few times throughout the following year. She was always generous with her time, her talents and her heart. About a month after I had spoken with her last, I received a parcel in the mail. The return address indicated that it was from the Exchange at Camp LeJeune. I opened it to find a beautiful shadow box filled with all of the medals and pins that Jason had earned. Each one had been mounted and displayed beautifully in the box along with Jason's rank and brass tags above each item indicating what each was for. There was also a brass plate that read: *LCPL Jason Redifer, United States Marine Corps, Semper Fidelis.* It was stunning! The box was a deep mahogany and was lined with black velvet. The entire display was almost breathtaking. I could feel something on the back as I was holding it so I turned it over to find a note:

> *27 June 2005*
> *Dear Mrs. Winfield,*
>
> *Hello again. I hope this letter finds you all well.*
> *As you probably already guessed, we've completed a "project" that began shortly after meeting you. A few ladies here in our Alteration Section are extremely talented and were able to put this display together.*
> *Please accept this shadowbox as our way of showing our respect, admiration, and appreciation to Jason.*
>
> *Semper Fideles,*
> *Jean E. Forte*
> *Military Clothing*
> *Sales Store*

I hope that in telling this story, she will know now the depth of what that gift has meant to me. Incredible women, incredible people, incredible Marines, incredible love.

At the luncheon, each family was assigned someone from within their child's unit that knew the deceased. This allowed each family to ask questions and possibly hear stories about their son's time in Iraq. We were treated to a lovely meal and I was extremely relieved when Major Moore came through the door. I felt like our connector to it all had arrived to plug us in.

After lunch, we were all introduced to the men responsible for the training and guidance of our sons. We were given a very informative briefing on the overall mission and objective accomplished there as well as very specific details of certain aspects. There was a question and answer session in which we were all encouraged to ask any questions we had.

I was so impressed by this entire process. First of all, I do not necessarily think that we needed to be privy to certain pieces of information. We were not Marines of the 24th MEU. The information we were being given was simply a courtesy. This was just a tool to help us to better understand and hopefully put some more of the pieces together. Secondly, they had to know the one question that would be on everyone's mind and it was no surprise when over and over again it came up. Why? Why did my son have to die?

I don't know how anyone can ever begin to answer that, and yet Colonel Johnson stood before these grieving families, some still raw with grief, and told them as honestly as he could the information that they sought. He provided visual aids to assist in putting the story of America's overall mission there in perspective as well as the mission of the 24th MEU. We were given detailed accounts of actual combat situations and accidents that claimed our loved ones lives.

I had no questions for the Colonel. I admired him greatly for openly inviting us all to this opportunity to persecute him and his team of leaders and openly hold them responsible for the deaths of our sons. I didn't feel this way but I knew that some of the others, lost in their grief, had to reach out for someone to blame.

The technical questions I had were all covered very thoroughly and Major Moore's visit had answered many other questions for me.

I just felt honored to be in a room full of men of such integrity, honor and pride. They had a belief in themselves, in their men, in their mission, in their job. They weren't afraid of the truth.

After the briefing, we were bussed to the parade field for the ceremony. We found our designated seats and our friends who had arrived to support us.

The entire 24th MEU, minus fifteen, (and several that were injured) were already assembled on the parade field. They were young, strong, uniform and powerful. The wind was blowing and the cool breeze caused my tears to sting my face. I looked out across that parade field and remembered the last time that I was seated at one.

It was August 29, 2003 at Parris Island, South Carolina. Jason had left for boot camp just two days after graduation from high school at age seventeen. He had enlisted just before Christmas of 2002 as an early enlistee. He was supposed to be joining the reserves so that he could still attend college. Apparently, Scott and I were the only ones who thought that. I signed for him to enlist after begging him to complete college first. He just kept telling me that he could always go to college and that it would be paid for after he enlisted in the Corps. This was something that he had to do now. Youthful ignorance is one thing, but the patriotic compassion in this young man was another.

Connie Davis, the school nurse at Stuart Hall, had desperately tried to talk Jason out of enlisting. She had come to know, love and admire Jason and was frightened for him. She told me not long after his death that she could still see the passion in his eyes and hear the conviction in his voice when he told her that she just didn't understand. He told her it was simply something he had to do. He emailed her a few days before his death telling her of another IED incident that he had been injured in. He said, "I told them I wanted Mrs. Davis to take care of me but they said they didn't think that would be possible."

She hated that he was there but came to understand, as we all did, that Jason simply had a calling and a mission long before he was branded a Marine and he had to answer that.

While we waited Christmas Eve dinner for Jason, I became impatient. He had gone to Richmond, Virginia the day before for military intake processing and was due home. He would later tell me that the officer doing the swearing in asked each of them why they were joining the armed forces. Jason said, "Sir, so my little brothers will be able to look at me with pride, Sir." He said the officer asked him to repeat what he just said and then got in his face and told him that he had better think of a reason for himself. Jason knew that his reason was for himself.

He bounded in full of excitement and enthusiasm and probably a little bit of fear. The thought of facing the enemy was one thing, the thought of facing your mother was another entirely. He lobbed out the information that he had not enlisted in the reserves but in fact, had gone full active duty, in the infantry, no less and would be leaving immediately following graduation. I thought I might faint. He was obviously not joking. I yelled something about him being insane and asked if he had a death wish. I suggested that rather than join the infantry I could just simply run him over with the car and be done with it! He found me very entertaining and somehow through my shock and anger he was able to see my pride.

We sat on the drill field in that suffocating August Parris Island heat. Anyone who has ever experienced the summertime there knows that it is a heat unlike anywhere else in the country. I have never before been so hot or so proud. I could spot Jason out of all of the recruits and our family all had on blue shirts with his name on them I cried as hard when my son was called "Marine" as I did when I held him for the very first time. Having not been able to attend Justin's graduation from Fort Leonard Wood, Michigan, when he became a military policeman for the Army, I was feeling it all for them both at this very moment. I had never known such pride in my entire life until I sat again at this parade field at Camp LeJeune because I had been forced to bury one of them.

The service began and I floated through most of it so overcome with grief and sadness that I thought I might just blow away. I held tightly to the stuffed Donkey that had come home in Jason's affects and a little stuffed monkey that I hadn't let go of since receiving his death notice. In fact, I cling to it still.

I will never forget the sharp penetration of the sound of the bagpipes, as the first notes of Amazing Grace pierced through my fog. I had tried to keep everything just on the periphery of focus so that I wouldn't completely give in to the emotional breakdown that was imminent. Once the lone bagpipe began its mournful wail I was jolted into a realm between here and the hereafter. Every lingering note screamed of my sorrow and my pain was carried across that field into the faces of every one of those young men. The silence broke the echo only long enough for another agonizing note to be cast to the wind. I was again raw and bleeding. How could something so beautiful be so painful? When at last the final note cried out, it resonated across us all for an eternity. Low, powerful, unending, complete.

Captain M. L. Brooks gave a final roll call. Each name of the deceased was read aloud. One by one the dead were listed. This would be the last time they would have to stand for accountability. My heart raced as he came to Jason's name. He read it and my blood seemed ready to spew forth from my body. I was ice cold and my heart was exploding beneath my sweater. I began to sweat and freeze at the same time. I could feel little dew drops on my skin yet my lips trembled and I couldn't speak.

Colonel Ron Johnson, the 24th MEU Commanding Officer, came forth for remarks. He stood before a group of sandbags that were placed evenly apart, fifteen in all. Each sandbag held an upside down rifle. Colonel Johnson walked the length of these bags and spoke of every young life that they represented. He knew each of them personally, if only because some were a constant face that he saw at mass every Sunday. One young man shared his birthday. One young man cried as he was bleeding to death, not because he was dying but because he felt he had let the Colonel down. He had a connection to them all.

When he approached the final three, he spoke of the incident that he said was the most painful for him. He recounted the mood of the entire MEU, as they were still "euphoric from the success of the elections." So close to over, so close to being home, these three died on the cusp of deliverance. It was this knowledge that seemed to sting him the most. He repeated each of their names as he spoke of them and hearing Jason's name from his lips evoked a strange sensation in me. It came so easily from him. It rolled off his tongue like it was so familiar. It hurt so much to hear it.

The honors detail was ordered forward and a small group marched up behind the sandbags. There were fifteen Marines across and several rows deep. Each sandbag had a group of Marines lined up behind it. In a series of well executed maneuvers, each Marine placed an object with the sandbag, turned and moved to the back of his line. The rifle had been placed bayonet side down into the bag and a Kevlar helmet would be hung on top of the other end of the rifle. A pair of combat boots would be placed in front of the rifle and a set of dog tags would be hung for each fallen Marine.

When they had completed their execution, they remained a formation within a formation and the firing detail readied themselves. My heart exploded as I heard the shots ring out. Each time, I jumped and each time I felt another piece of my heart splinter off. As the smoke from the rifles cleared the haunting sound of Taps began. Another bugle. Another day. The marking of another dead. Day is done.

As the final note dissipated into the air the service was concluded and we all began to unfold from under the tents in which we had been seated. I began walking toward the display that represented Jason, and Amanda joined me. The Marines who had created the display were excused. All but one Marine at each post, who stood guard.

We stood before that representation and I just could not believe that this was what had become of my son. From behind a waterfall of tears, silent, uneventful tears, I reached out to touch the dog tags. I asked the Marine guard if I could take them. He reverently indicated that I could and I pulled them gently off the rifle and handed them to Amanda. She started to tell me no and resist and I just closed her hand around them and whispered, "Yes."

I looked at the Donkey in my hand and I could hear Jason making those silly voices. How unjust that this was all I had.

As I started to walk back to my family, I saw Sergeant Craft. He was the Marine who recruited Jason. My mother had seen him a few times back home before Jason was killed and angrily told him that she held him responsible for Jason's safety. She was worried sick about him and she was going to hold Sergeant Craft accountable. Obviously not being a stranger to devoted grandmothers, he simply explained that Jason was well trained to do his job and that he would be fine. He wasn't fine now.

I prayed that my mother did not make a visual on Sergeant Craft and swoop in for the attack before I could head her off. I knew that her pain was driving her but I also knew that Sergeant Craft would be dealing with his own pain.

He met me half way and we tried to look at each other without looking at each other. Eye to eye was too raw and revealing. We both had tears that we wanted to hide from the other. We both had pride and courage and we both needed each other more than we knew.

I just jumped in and interrupted his pleasantries. "Don't you dare hold yourself responsible for this. Jason would have been a Marine whether you would have been the one to push the paperwork or not. How he got into the Corps is insignificant, he LOVED being a Marine and he was more proud of that fact than of anything in his life, except his family. You led him to an opportunity to be the man that he was born to be. Don't you ever be ashamed of that."

I felt like I was telling Maverick that he had to get back up there and fly. Goose would want it that way. It was a little "Top Gun" even as it was coming out of my mouth and I almost smiled at one point. I think that was Jason.

I did find my mother on my way to the bus. She had been talking with a group of Jason's friends. When I got to her she was visibly rattled. I would soon learn that she had been asking for certain details from anyone who had actually witnessed the attack. She still had questions. She still needed answers. While I never wanted her to cause these young men to have to relive such a horrific event, I was stunned to know what she had discovered.

I now knew the truth. I had the solution to the mystery from Major Moore's visit. I knew what he had left unspoken that day. I now had questions that could only be answered at home.

Jason's body had been severed in two. The account from the vehicle directly behind his was that in the explosion, a piece of the vehicle had apparently cut him in half. They said there was very little blood at all, but that he was just a torso. Imagine that of your child.

After my horror in hearing the facts, I quickly rebounded to ask, then just how he came to be in unrecognizable pieces. I was fully aware that the climate was very hot and that smaller explosions continued to go off, etc., etc. But Major Moore had choked on the words; "he was definitely recognizable."

The stories didn't match up and I had obviously been deceived. I was headed home for my answers. Someone was going to explain to me why I had been robbed of my last chance to hold my child. Someone was going to be very surprised that something they thought was dead and buried was about to rise again.

As we passed through the gates of Camp LeJeune for what I thought would be the last time, I couldn't help but feel yet another loss that we would never return. We no longer belonged. We were no longer part of that "special city." With sadness, emptiness, anger and regret we headed home. Camp LeJeune had held a wonderful memorial and had given much to us in our loss. I would always be thankful and would always miss this place.

CHAPTER 10

ANSWERS

The nightmares overwhelmed me until I was afraid to sleep. I would see Jason riding along, thinking of coming home and suddenly being blown in half. The images were so vivid. I could hear his voice scream out, "Ma" as he was ripped in two. I could smell smoke and the putrid stench of burning flesh. I could hear the explosions all around me and men yelling from a distance. I could feel my own insides pouring out into the street and when I would awaken, I would look at my hands for the blood I had felt all over them and cry for the emptiness because I was not holding him.

I went to speak with the funeral director immediately. I told him that I had just returned from a memorial service at Camp LeJeune and that I had received some information that was quite disturbing. I told him I had some questions about Jason's body that I needed to have answered. While becoming increasingly more uncomfortable, he assured me he would answer any questions that I had.

As I began, he interrupted to ask just where this information had come from. He was fishing and trying to determine where I was going before he was put in the hot seat. No, sir. I had trusted once. I ignored his request and simply asked if he could recount for me the condition of Jason's remains.

Silence. Discomfort filled the room and he was completely unsure what I wanted and what I expected. Furthermore, he was completely unsure of what I knew.

He basically began with some vague recounting and I immediately tried to pin it down. We verbally danced for a little while until I became restless. He was more interested in trying to figure out where the information had come from that was fueling my inquiry than he was to just directly answer what was posed to him.

He reminded me of the weather conditions of the climate in Iraq. The length of time in which it took to get the body home. The fact that Dover did not expect anyone would be viewing the body and had therefore certainly skipped certain procedures that would have been purely cosmetic and last but not least, that if my concerns were being raised because of something one of Jason's comrades may have said, then I should rest assured that all was well because both time and trauma would have a way of obscuring what they would remember, thereby nullifying any accounts by accident witnesses.

After a few seconds of letting him babble in this regard we cut to the chase. My friend, Avis, had driven me over and was by my side yet again. When she could no longer stand his direct avoidance of my question, she interrupted by asking, "did you see his face?"

He was stunned. He admitted, with much reluctance, that he had not but that it was probable that we would not have been able to recognize it.

I was paralyzed. This meant that there was a head. There was probably a face. There was probably an entire torso, just as we had come to learn. There was no bag of "parts" that was completely unrecognizable.

I could have held my baby. I could have stroked his precious cheek. I could have run my fingers through his beautiful, shiny black hair. I could have clipped a lock of his hair to keep.

Did I expect him to look like the child of mine that left here that June day? Of course not! But discoloration, swelling, loss of blood, etc. That would still have been my child and no one will ever make me believe now that I would not have known him.

I will never know how I drew another breath. I was absolutely flattened. I stood up immediately and thanked him for his time, briefly mumbled something about not making that decision for another mother ever again and left.

I understand why he did it. I believe that in his mind he thought he was doing the right thing for me. It was not, however, his decision to make. He will never know what he has robbed from me and we are both powerless to change it.

Avis and I decided that at least we had answers. At least I could stop battling with the confusions that haunted me because none of the facts added up. Now, at least I knew. Now, I would have to learn to live with it.

I learned immediately after leaving Camp LeJeune that Jason would be receiving the Navy and Marine Corps Achievement Medal posthumously. Major Moore said that he would be honored to come up and present it whenever we would like. We knew that a presentation was scheduled in our little community park for a flagpole and some benches in Jason's honor and we hoped that he could come for that.

The Stuarts Draft Post Office had spearheaded a movement to have this area erected and dedicated to Jason. They were all dear friends that I had worked with over the years and they had basically watched my children grow up. They all remembered the day Jason rode his horse over and was waiting for me in the parking lot and they had all had to listen to my tales about the boys, both good and bad, for years. My friend, Ruby Barnett, said she immediately turned to their postmaster and suggested putting up some benches the day after they learned of the news.

The Stuarts Draft Veterans of Foreign Wars had the flag poles set and placed a marker in Jason's name at the site dedicating it to him. There is a bench placed there by the Post Office and one by the Stuarts Draft Ruritans. Trees and plants are provided by area businesses and it is truly a place of beauty.

Especially since Jason was placed in Arlington for burial, this area has become sacred to us as a place to go in memory. My mother visits almost every single day and keeps it decorated for the season and for special dates to our family. I know that I don't have to go anywhere to talk to him but it is nice to have a designated place close by to honor him.

The VFW organized a dedication and Major Moore planned to attend to make the presentation of the award. On June 14, 2005, we assembled for the ceremony.

It was a beautiful summer evening and many of our family and friends attended. The mountains in the background provided a picturesque backdrop as they always do and the sound of the flags being raised up the poles with the wind catching them was musical. I love the crisp snapping of the flags as they are buffeted around. The sky was almost purple and there was so much love around us that evening that it was palpable.

The VFW played "God Bless the USA" and we all cried. Our friend, John Nuckolls, gave a few personal words as Jason and John's wife Janet had become fast pen pals while he was gone. She had just retired from the post office and Jason had promised her that he would be home for her retirement party. She knew that death would have been the only thing to have kept him from it.

Our immediate family was then escorted to the memorial stone. While we stood there Major Moore was introduced and he read the citation and presented the Achievement Medal. When he read off some of Jason's accomplishments I was shocked. I had no way of knowing all that he had done in Iraq. I am sure I never will. When we talked on the phone we tried to talk of home and our love for one another and converse in a way that seemed familiar and familial to him. He never had time to "talk shop." He only wanted to discuss "the important things" in his life.

Major Moore read:
"THIS IS TO CERTIFY THAT THE SECRETARY OF THE NAVY HAS AWARDED THE NAVY AND MARINE CORPS ACHIEVEMENT MEDAL TO LANCE CORPORAL JASON C. REDIFER, UNITED STATES MARINE CORPS, FOR PROFESSIONAL ACHIEVEMENT WHILE SERVING AS DESIGNATED MARKSMAN AND RIFLEMAN, 2nd

PLATOON, COMPANY A, BATTALION LANDING TEAM, 1st BATTALION, 2nd MARINES, 24TH MARINE EXPEDITIONARY UNIT IN SUPPORT OF OPERATION IRAQI FREEDOM II FROM 23 JULY 2004 TO 31 JANUARY, 2005. LANCE CORPORAL REDIFER DISPLAYED DETERMINATION AND COURAGE IN PURSUIT OF MISSION ACCOMPLISHMENT. HE CONDUCTED CORDON AND SEARCH OPERATIONS, VEHICLE CHECKPOINTS, AND WAS IN OVER ONE HUNDRED TWENTY COMBAT PATROLS TO GAIN SECURITY AND PREVENT INDIRECT FIRE AND IMPROVISED EXPLOSIVE DEVICE ATTACKS ON COALITION FORCES. ON 9 AUGUST, 2004, ENEMY FORCES ATTACKED HIS PATROL WITH TWO IMPROVISED EXPLOSIVE DEVICES CAUSING CASUALTIES. WITHOUT HESITATION, HE IDENTIFIED AND SECURED A HELICOPTER LANDING ZONE TO EVACUATE WOUNDED MARINES. ON NUMEROUS OCCASIONS, HE EMPLOYED SKILLS AS A DESIGNATED MARKSMAN AND SERVED AS GUARDIAN ANGEL FOR HIS FELLOW MARINES. HIS EFFORTS ASSISTED IN MAKING THE AREA OF OPERATIONS A MORE STABLE AND SECURE ENVIRONMENT TO SUPPORT THE FIRST FREE ELECTIONS IN IRAQ. LANCE CORPORAL REDIFER'S COURAGE, TENACIOUS ATTITUDE, AND DEVOTION TO DUTY REFLECTED CREDIT UPON HIMSELF AND WERE IN KEEPING WITH THE HIGHEST TRADITIONS OF THE MARINE CORPS AND THE UNITED STATES NAVAL SERVICE. GIVEN THIS 1ST DAY OF APRIL 2005 BY R.T.DURKIN, LIEUTENANT COLONEL, U.S. MARINE CORPS, COMMANDING OFFICER.

The citation had further information, which read:
SUMMARY OF ACTION-THIS IS A POSTHUMOUS AWARD
Lance Corporal Jason C. Redifer is enthusiastically recommended for the Navy and Marine Corps Achievement Medal for professional achievement while assigned as Designated Marksman and Rifleman, 2d Platoon, Company A, Battalion Landing Team, 1st Battalion, 2nd Marines, 24th Marine Expeditionary Unit, 23 July to 31 January 2005.
The area of operations assigned to Battalion Landing Team (BLT), 1st Battalion, 2nd Marines in the northern Babil Province was known as an

extremely volatile area due to the large amount of improvised explosive devices and heavy insurgent activity. The primary mission for the BLT was to protect the critical infrastructure in the area. This infrastructure included a power plant, power lines, oil pipelines, bridges, a main supply route, and an alternate supply route. Overall security in the assigned area was initially very poor and enemy attacks focused on the Iraqi Security Forces, Coalition Forces, Iraqi Police stations, and Multi-National Force contractors operating in the area. Through six months of demanding, sustained combat operations, Lance Corporal Redifer displayed superb dedication in the execution of his duties and assisted in the overall success of the BLT. Arriving in Iraq, the BLT was positioned inside a power plant compound at Camp Iskandariyah, Iraq and was subjected to indirect fire attacks almost daily. In addition, improvised explosive device (IED) attacks were directed at the BLT's patrols on a daily basis and occurred as many as five to six times a day. Lance Corporal Redifer's variety of tasks included conducting counter-mortar, counter-IED, and security patrols in addition to serving as a member of the BLT's Quick Reaction Force for almost three months. During his time in Iraq, he participated in numerous cordon and search operations, vehicle checkpoint operations, and over one hundred and twenty combat patrols. Due to the vast area of operations and large number of tasks assigned to the battalion, his patrols sometimes lasted over twelve hours. Through his stamina, devotion to duty, and tenacious attitude, Lance Corporal Redifer no doubt assisted in ensuring a more stable and secure environment in the area of operations.

Lance Corporal Redifer always displayed his ability to adapt to any task he faced. Arriving in Iraq, the company was transformed into a motorized rifle company utilizing up-armored highly mobile multipurpose-wheeled vehicles (HMMWV). Due to the number of required driver's,

Lance Corporal Redifer was chosen as a new HMMWV driver. Because the area was filled with unimproved canal roads, drivers were forced to operate both day and night on unfamiliar, hazardous terrain. Lance Corporal Redifer perfected his driving skills in record time. His skillful handling of this difficult vehicle was recognized and he was assigned the duty of being his platoon commander's driver. Observing his abilities left no doubt in his platoon commander's mind that Lance Corporal Redifer would be able to handle the difficult driving assignment with the ease of a professional.

On 9 August 2004, Lance Corporal Redifer's mechanized patrol was attacked by two simultaneous IEDs along alternate supply route San Juan just west of the Euphrates River. Immediately following the attack, Lance Corporal Redifer recognized that several Marines were wounded in the explosion. He took the initiative and assembled several Marines for security, identified a potential helicopter-landing zone, notified his platoon commander, and secured the site. His quick thinking and decisive actions enabled the casualties to be evacuated in a timely and efficient manner.

Lance Corporal Redifer's duties extended beyond that of the average rifleman. Prior to the deployment, he was recognized as an expert marksman. His shooting abilities earned him the position of the platoon's designated marksman. He quickly perfected these skills and ensured his weapon was meticulously maintained and ready for action. In addition to his shooting skills, he diligently learned all immediate action drills performed by the platoon in order to best support his fellow Marines under any circumstance. On countless occasions, Lance Corporal Redifer provided his critical expertise in observation and marksmanship as a Guardian Angel for the Marines around him. In the dangerous environment he was faced with, he utilized his scope to *provide additional situational awareness to his fellow Marines and give them accurate and timely reporting on their surroundings.*

Following a successful Iraqi election on 30 January 2005, Lance Corporal Redifer was conducting a patrol on the afternoon of 31 January 2005. The patrol's mission was to provide security for the BLT's forward operating base (FOB) and deter enemy mortar attacks against the FOB to which he was assigned. The patrol was moving south along a heavily attacked route near the Euphrates River when they were attacked with an IED. The force of the IED destroyed the vehicle Lance Corporal Redifer was riding in, wounding two Marines and killing three Marines instantly, including Lance Corporal Redifer.

Lance Corporal Redifer was dedicated in every aspect of his duties. Serving in a hostile area as an infantryman, he was subjected to almost daily indirect fire, direct fire, and improvised explosive device attacks. His subordinates, peers, and superiors alike admired his devotion to duty and fearless attitude. Throughout sustained combat operations, Lance Corporal Redifer was an inspiration to his platoon. His total dedication to mission accomplishment assisted in creating a safe environment for the local citizens to vote in their first free Iraqi election. His courage and determination in mission success are deserving of special recognition.

After Major Moore had finished, we were presented with an Honorary Membership for Jason into the Stuarts Draft VFW. He wanted so much to come home and join their ranks. I was very honored to receive this as well.

The memorial stone was now unveiled and the VFW played "Some Gave All" which landed us all in tears again.

My friend from the post office and member of the VFW, Butch Bentley, gave a beautiful prayer and once again we listened to Taps.

Charles Weaver, the Post Commander of Post 9339, had told us that this Veterans Memorial would serve to pay tribute to the countless number of men and women who have stood and continue to stand ready to guard our freedom every day of their lives. He said we should never forget the price our veterans, past and present, have paid for our freedom. He said, "the men and women of the VFW have stood the line, have known the sting of battle, and the memories that linger a lifetime."

As he looked upon the flags he said, "A great American once expressed it well in an address to West Point cadets by saying, 'Duty, Honor, Country, This is what our flag symbolizes'. So, if you get a lump in your throat and a tear in your eye each time you see Old Glory, you are not alone. You are an American."

I have had a tear in my eye and lump in my throat every time I have seen those beautiful flags and felt the love, respect, honor and dedication of friends, comrades and fellow Americans that dwells in that spot.

I had received an email when we had returned from Camp LeJeune that had a photo attached. Christopher Zimny's dad was able to retrieve a photo of Jason from Chris' camera. Apparently, Corporal Zimny had been keeping a photo journal of his time in Iraq and the last picture he had the opportunity to take was of Jason less than five minutes before the attack. I have no idea how this tiny digital camera survived this type of destruction. I believe it was purely a little gift from God. One last moment of life captured.

As I scrolled up the email and Jason's face came into view, I was stunned. It was so difficult to see how tired he looked and imagine how he was thinking about just getting through one last patrol to come home. It was almost impossible to process that just moments after the snapshot was taken he was blown in half. The picture was the worst piece of reality I had experienced and yet was a treasure because it was truly the last of him that had been there.

As I sat on the post office bench later that night, all alone, I thought of that picture. I listened to the new, crisp flags fluttering in the gentle summer night and the sounds of the crickets singing a little nighttime lullaby just for me. I thought of Jason's pains and glories. I thought of my own.

Justin and I had recently each gotten tattoos in honor of Jason. It was a first for both of us and quite unexpected for a mother of almost forty to do! It seemed understandable that Justin might do such a thing but when he talked about it, I was filled with an urgency to do something so significant as well. I wanted my pain and grief to somehow be visible on my outside in a way that would partially give a window to how I had been branded on the inside. We talked over several ideas and though we felt utterly ridiculous arranging a mother/son tattoo session. The woman named Margaret who saw us didn't seem to find this the least bit unusual. She was so kind and sympathetic to our situation.

Justin had his entire back done and Margaret was very impressed that he embarked on such a large project his first time out of the gate. She thought his stamina was remarkable as she finished four intense hours of inking. I was glad he went first so I would know what to expect. She assured us that tattooing was addictive. I pray I never have another reason to go back.

I can honestly say that the burning pain felt almost good at first. It was something I could at least feel. I hadn't realized how numb I had become. When I would feel it was a little too intense, I would look up at Justin who was encouraging me. I would glance up from the table into his eyes and they were saying, "it's O.K., it's for Jason."

I understand now what a good pain is. It was extreme at times, barely noticeable at times. It was about the son I lost and the son before me who was feeling the same pain.

Two hours after I lay down on Margaret's table, I was finished. I had a beautiful tattoo that was a much smaller version of Justin's. We were now both marked with that vision that had burned itself into my mind that day in North Carolina. Now it was burned into my skin. The sandbags, the rifle, the helmet, the boots, the dog tags. Behind the rifle was a set of crossed flags, a U.S. Marine Corps flag and an American flag. The banner above reads "MY HERO, MY SON, MY SOUL." The banner below says, "LCPL JASON REDIFER."

I sat on that bench, that balmy June night and saw all of these things in my mind. I prayed that later when I would lay down my head, that I would do so without fear, without nightmares. Please God let the love of the dear friends who gave us this holy place for refuge fill us and push away the evil that had settled into my nights. By the way, tell Jason I miss him terribly.

CHAPTER 11

AN INTERNATIONAL STORY

Chris Graham of the Augusta Free Press, a local online newspaper, contacted me before Christmas of 2004. He had learned of Jason while visiting Stuart Hall and wanted to do a piece on him. He set up an appointment and came to my house and we visited for hours. He began the interview by asking me some basic questions and quickly we were old friends talking about my son's tour of duty in Iraq. He met Courtland and Carter and took a photo of us in front of our Christmas tree holding a large picture of Jason in his dress blues. The story would be called, "I'll be home for Christmas."

I really enjoyed Chris' visit and loved having the chance to share family stories with him. He said that he would enjoy emailing Jason and would like to talk with him in person when he came home and do a follow up story. He never had that opportunity.

He has told me since that as he went out our driveway that day, he called his wife, Crystal. He was telling her about his experience at our house and suddenly he had a foreboding feeling sweep over him. He remembered thinking how horrible it would be if his next visit to our home would not be in celebration. He prayed that would not be the case.

We have spent much time together since that day. In my inability to form rational thought or to even sleep the night we were given the news, I went to the computer to email Chris. I just thought he needed to know that his story was over. At 10:43pm on January 31st, I wrote:

> Dear Chris
>   I am writing to let you know that we received notice today that Jason died in Iraq this morning due to an IED bomb. As you can imagine, we are

devastated. I wanted to take a moment to let you know because you were so kind and concerned and we all really appreciated the article you did on Jason at Christmas. He told me that he had received emails from you and looked very forward to speaking with you in person when he came home.

I spoke with him a couple of hours before his death. He was headed out on his final mission. He was due to come home on 2/9/05. I am sorry you will not have the opportunity to talk with him in person but know that he was honored by your article and appreciated mostly the fact that you had spent time with me and his brothers.

> *Sincerely*
> *Rhonda L. Winfield*

Chris replied to me at 10:54pm, although it would be weeks before I would read it:

Rhonda

My heart sank tonight when I heard on the evening news that three Marines had died today in Iraq. As with other stories of this nature, my thoughts turned immediately to Jason and praying that he was safe. I am so sorry for you and your family-particularly for Jason's little brothers, whom I had the pleasure of meeting, and whom I know so looked up to their big brother.

I know that there might not be much that I can do-but please, if there is anything, let me know. I never had the fortune of meeting Jason-but through you, I felt as if I had been privileged to get to know him, at least a little bit.

> *My prayers are with you,*
> *Chris Graham*

Chris has continued to tell Jason's story and has worked tirelessly to keep his memory alive. He has covered not only all of the events surrounding the funeral, burial, etc., but has done stories for every holiday, birthday, anniversary, etc.

Chris was contacted during early July by a reporter from the British Broadcasting Corporation. Chris checked his credentials and then forwarded on his information to me. His name was Matthew Davis and he was out of the Washington D.C. office. He wanted to do an article for BBC online. After I received his email request, I yelled into our kitchen and read it to Scott.

"Do you suppose BBC means THE BBC?" I questioned. We decided it must be since we could think of nothing else! I had done an interview a couple of weeks after Jason's death for National Public Radio but this was international!

I agreed to do the interview and we wrote back and forth for a couple of weeks. He became caught up in California during the Michael Jackson child molestation trial and when he returned we set a date.

I had been putting off taking Jason's uniform to Stuart Hall. I was certainly not having any second thoughts about doing it, it was just so hard to assemble those things and go through everything that it would require emotionally. I had decided that I could either leave the uniform hanging in his closest where it would just age and maybe I would come in and rub my hands across it periodically, or I could send it to the school where it could be seen and admired every day. Jason would have been so proud to think that it was there as a symbol of the ideals that he valued so highly. I also decided that I would donate his Marine Corps ring and his Stuart Hall class ring. He was so proud of both. I certainly couldn't wear them and they seemed to compliment the uniform.

Mr. Davis had indicated that he would like to talk to a couple of Jason's friends and perhaps some of the people at Stuart Hall. I let everyone know when he was to arrive and the interview literally took on a life of its own.

I am sure it would be very difficult to come speak to someone who had lost her child. Finding the right things to say is difficult enough when you know the person you are talking to. In this case, he didn't know me at all and he was trying to find a way to delicately ask me some difficult questions. I could tell immediately that he

117

wasn't quite sure just how to tread and that moment of hesitation probably threw whatever he had tentatively planned right out the window.

I met him and suggested that we go to the Stuarts Draft Park to Jason's memorial. I wanted him to see what the members of our community had worked so hard on and put so much of themselves into to honor one of their own. I wanted him to see that Jason was not just special to me. After having done countless interviews by this point with radio, newspaper and television I knew the drill and fell into pattern. He seemed a little surprised when I positioned myself, began telling him the setup and waited for him to retrieve his camera from the car.

After we left the memorial, we went to our house where we spent a great deal of time in Jason's room. I was able to show him the countless letters, cards, flags and gifts from all over that had been sent to us, most by people we have never met.

Tammy came over and Mr. Davis had an opportunity to interview her as someone who had known Jason most of his life.

One of Jason's best friends, Josh Lotts, came over for an interview as well. Josh was the friend that Jason left his horse to. Josh is still so emotional over the loss of Jason that he can barely speak of it, but he wanted Jason's story to be presented, at least in part, by someone who understood his cowboy heart. Josh was embarrassed that he was unable to put more of his thoughts into words. He had no idea the simple eloquence of what he had said of his friend. His words conveyed a love, a respect and a loss far greater than many will ever know. He did a beautiful job.

After these interviews, I gathered up the uniform and all the things that went along with it and we headed to Stuart Hall.

School was out, as this was the beginning of August, but the faculty assembled en masse. They all loved Jason and wanted to make sure the whole world knew so. Jason's friend and school nurse, who he had asked for in

Iraq, was there as well. Connie Davis would have taken a bullet herself for him and she was there leading the horde.

Mr. Davis had all the opportunity he wanted to speak with people representing the school, in fact probably much more than he wanted! Afterward, I did my best to hand over the uniform without becoming very emotional. This was no formal ceremony, it was simply a handoff and I thought with all the distraction I would be able to get through it.

I noticed as I was pulling it from the garment bag that I hadn't placed Jason's qualifying pin for marksmanship on it. He had qualified as expert and I didn't know what all I should include for this.

Josh, who had come along, slipped over to the office to call the local recruiting office to ask. Less that fifteen minutes later, Josh returned with the Marine that ran the office. He had come over to help us out and to present me with a very special gift.

He had just taken over the office and in cleaning things out he found something that he thought needed to be returned to me. I couldn't imagine what he could have and as anticipation was getting the best of me, he pulled from behind his back a red plastic folder. I opened it to find Jason's Stuart Hall diploma inside.

I had never thought to miss it. He had left for boot camp just three days after graduation and I had never even had the chance to see it up close. Sergeant Craft, the recruiter at the time, had attended Jason's graduation and took the diploma with him immediately afterward to finish some final paperwork for processing. I suppose it had remained at the office all this time.

I was so thrilled to have it. Who knows how long it could have been before I ever wondered where it was. Who knows how many hours of frustration would have been spent trying to locate it at home if I had thought of it!

I looked at Connie, who was crying by now along with me, and knew that this too would need to remain at Stuart Hall.

Since I had already started with the tears, I just went ahead and handed over the uniform and the rings. I had taken his hat, his shoes and even his socks along as well as part of the uniform because we still didn't know exactly what type of display they would have. When I pulled his gloves out of the bag, I could hold nothing else back. They still had a little dirt on the underside of the fingertips where he had worn them last. It was in that very building that he had them on for the final time. He had returned home for the graduation of another class and was so proud to be able to go in his uniform. He had returned home to make the family proud; this time it was his Stuart Hall family. I warbled through my sobs that I just couldn't make myself have them cleaned. Every time I thought about it, it just seemed like I was washing away the last traces of his presence. I handed them to Connie dirty and told her that they would need to have someone do it.

She said that they would remain exactly as they were.

Poor Mr. Davis, I am quite sure he had never banked on all of this.

He did a lovely article and I couldn't help but feel like perhaps his experience that day had changed him somehow.

After the article ran, I emailed a copy to Lieutenant Mark Nicholson, Jason's platoon officer in Alpha Company. I hoped he would share it with some of the others who knew and served with Jason.

I met Lieutenant Nicholson while I was visiting Jamel once at Walter Reed. Justin was with me and we were hanging out with Jamel while he finished a physical therapy session. It was the day he let me pick the color of his wheelchair.

We didn't know that Lieutenant Nicholson would be there and he certainly wasn't expecting us. Justin and I walked around a corner looking for Jamel and Lieutenant Nicholson was standing there. When he saw us his face went absolutely white. I knew immediately that he had seen Jason in Justin's face.

We made quick introductions and had a wonderful opportunity to visit with him that day as well. He shared some pictures and stories with me and we felt all the richer for our encounter.

As I forwarded the BBC article to him, I hoped he would remember who I was. He replied later,

Dear Ms. Winfield, of course I remember you. Thank you for remembering me. I thought the BBC story honored Jason and portrayed him exactly how he lived; an honorable and brave young man who served his country and fellow Marines with courage and enthusiasm. I think about Jason, Chris and Harry on a daily basis. How they made me laugh, how they impressed me as brave men and how they made me work hard to ensure I did the best job I could because I loved every one of them. I have so many fond memories of Jason that it brings a smile to my face every time I think of him and at the same time it breaks my heart to know I didn't bring him home to you. He reminds me to train this new group of Marines to the utmost of my abilities because they deserve everything I have and more. Jason was my driver and I knew him closely. Whenever it was 3rd Squads turn to patrol, I went to Sergeant Augustine and told him I wanted LCPL Redifer to drive for me. I knew he was a good ol' country boy and that he knew how to drive. I used to tell him, "Red, drive like you always wanted to at home but were never allowed to" and he would say, "Roger that, sir" in his unmistakable country accent. I would just smile with confidence and tell him, "Let's go get into something." I also remember the joke going around 2nd platoon when Jason showed everyone the picture of his brother and they all thought it was me. The truth is, when I met Jason's brother, I almost fell over. I knew exactly who you were before anyone introduced us. I knew he was Jason's brother. I couldn't even look at him for fear I would break down and cry right in front of you. I can't imagine the pain you still feel from losing Jason. I wish that I had some grand thoughts of wisdom concerning your loss, but I don't. Just know that I share that loss with you...everyday. I swear to you and to all the mothers of the sons under my command that I will do the best of my abilities to ensure those boys are properly trained, equipped, led and ready to fight. Tomorrow, we head out to sea for 3 weeks of training on the ships that will take us once again into harms way. It was my privilege to lead your son in this war for freedom and democracy. I am a better man because of it and I will never forget the time I spent with him. You, along with Jason, Chris and Harry are in my daily thoughts and prayers. Please take care and know that Jason is still driving for me.

Lieutenant Mark Nicolson
Alpha Co. 1st BN 2nd Marines

It is an indescribable comfort to know that in many ways Jason will always be with him. His letter is one that I have read many, many times and am sure I will continue to do so.

Another correspondence that I can not get enough of is an email that Jason sent Scott from Iraq. He sent a photo of himself and was so proud that he had learned how to do so. He was just checking in and wanted to make sure Scott showed me the photo so I could see proof that he was well. We were both shocked to see it.

Scott says that to this day he remembers that as being the defining moment for him in the realization that Jason was, in fact, a man.

It was the first glimpse of him that we had since he left us. He was so changed. He was so old, so weathered, and so tough. He was not our child or even the man we saw him emerging into before he left. Of course, he had always been a "little grown-up" but this photo depicted someone who had undergone a transformation of an enormous magnitude. He was not our Jason. He was a warrior. His eyes were deep and dark in a way I had never known possible. They were eyes that had seen life vanish from other eyes.   He was a machine set on survival mode.

I saw that day that he was technically "all right" as he had hoped that I would.   I also saw someone that I had never known and prayed that the faint light of Jason that I knew was there would once again illuminate his soul.

We never saw another picture of him until after his death. It was his last email home.

CHAPTER 12

THE RALLY

It was the time of year when evenings were filled with funnel cakes, corn dogs and blue ribbon peaches. It was county fair season. Our fair had been a fledgling effort that was growing each year but still at the point where it needed every person's attendance and support. We had been planning to go for a couple of days and Scott was insisting that we actually make it there this time. The boys were excited and had been looking forward to it. I was dragging my feet and I knew it was because I would have to encounter people that we had not conversed with since Jason's death. I didn't want to go. I didn't want to think about being there last year and how many things had changed in such a short amount of time.

Like most days now, I reminded myself that I didn't have the luxury of curling up in bed and crying about it. Courtland and Carter loved the county fair and of course, Jason would have made sure that they had the opportunity to go. So, I was gathering steam and as I finished getting ready I turned on the evening news while waiting for Scott.

The coverage took my legs out from under me and I dropped to the couch to catch my breath. She had gone too far. This was the straw that had broken the camel's back.

Like most of the rest of the country, I had been watching Cindy Sheehan wage a protest on President Bush and the Iraq war by camping outside of his Crawford, Texas ranch. While I didn't agree with her politics, I certainly couldn't fault her for voicing her opinions. I had been discussing her ideas and actions with a friend earlier in the week. O.K., I was actually venting about what I considered to be a ridiculous stunt depicting what I believed to be yet another misled American who had obviously followed the path of war as was laid down by the American media!   It seemed that the more information I gained on this woman, the more ridiculous her situation seemed. I could not believe, for instance, that her son had volunteered for TWO tours of duty! I was sure he was turning over in his grave watching his mother renounce the fundamental American values that were surely at the heart of every soldier and Marine! During this mini rant, my friend, who also had like views, simply reminded me that Jason didn't die buying the right to speak one's mind only if you agreed with his view.   He paid in blood to purchase that right for every single American.   The message was so simple and so true. So O.K., I couldn't fault her for voicing her views, no matter how skewed, in my opinion, but I was certainly tired of seeing the situation escalate each day and the media attention was growing in like proportion.   It annoyed me, got under my skin and then the afternoon came when it simply boiled my blood.

A display had been erected in Crawford as part of Cindy's protest and attempt to gain audience with the president. There were individual crosses bearing the names of every fallen service member who had given their lives in Iraq. I fully understood that the facts were not in dispute and that Jason was part of that count. Fair enough. He was, however, NOT part of the Cindy Sheehan movement or anything that it stood for. I listened in horror as she presented the display and basically told America that she spoke as the moral voice of the war. She was a mother who had lost a son and every one of those crosses not only represented a life lost but also a suffering mother. She was the lone voice of these grieving, broken mothers and together we were begging our president to bring home our troops immediately and insure that no other mothers would have to mourn the loss that we were unable to now escape. This, at least, was the message I heard and I thought I might actually have a stroke.

By the time Scott bounded into the house, anxious to clean up and head off to the fair, I was in a bonafide meltdown. After about an hour of emotional explosion directed toward a man whose only error was to not come back early enough for me to have missed this news coverage, I was finally able to take a deep breath. Trying to be a trooper and feeling guilty for dumping on Scott, I sucked it all up temporarily and announced that since I had vented, I would be able to go on to the fair. We gathered up the family and drove on over.

Though I had been initially stubborn in leaving the house, it was turning out to be a nice retreat from our sadness. The children had a great time and even though I was still feeling like I was the man behind the curtain in the Wizard of Oz, I was basically doing well. Everyone kept focus on the Great Oz, admiring my strength and faith and no one seemed to have a clue that just beyond sight was a broken, pathetic, shell of a person that may not ever stand on her own two feet again. So, I was keeping up the charade and in the course of all that work, actually managed to feel glad that we had brought the children. It was great to hear them laugh and have fun. I knew that even though my best acting efforts were given for their benefit, they knew that I wasn't really in the game like I pretended to be. They knew Mom was gone but were happy to have what was left, at least.

When we had finally spent the last of our energy, as well as the last of our money, we began working our way to the parking lot. We decided to stroll through an exhibit building that we had missed earlier on the way. I immediately ran into a few friends that were working a booth for the Augusta County Republicans and one of them nonchalantly asked me what I thought of the recent Cindy Sheehan news coverage. Scott looked like he had been struck by a bolt of lightning and herded the children quickly to another booth to seek shelter before 'Tornado Rhonda' touched down again. By the time I had finished I had not only raised my blood pressure by at least twenty points but had unwittingly organized a rally.

My friend, Lynn Mitchell, who had launched the hailstorm of emotion at the fair, emailed me the next evening with a news release for my approval inviting everyone to come join me on the courthouse steps the following weekend for a rally in support of our troops. Game on!

When I started thinking about what I may want to actually say, I couldn't help but get sidetracked by my thoughts toward Cindy Sheehan and those crosses. I knew that she had every right to display those names. It was factual that they were casualties of this war. I HATED that by doing so, she was giving the impression that she was speaking for their now silent voices. I believed she could be representing the opinions of some parents and families left behind but she did not speak for me or mine. I also kept thinking about how she was referred to as "anti-war." Did that make me "pro-war" by default? I just thought it made me "pro-American."

I didn't WANT war. I wanted a country where my children could feel safe and not be murdered by terrorists on their way to school.

I had listened to her demand that President Bush order all the troops home immediately. Did that not mean that both of our sons would have given their lives in vain? No matter what anyone thought now about entering the war, we had to finish the job. Surely, this was not a matter of party lines? For God sake! Grief is bipartisan! I was thinking that we ALL want our troops home as quickly as possible. Why couldn't we just pray for their accelerated advance to victory instead of their rapid withdrawal to defeat?

That's when I decided to just write her a letter.

Dear Cindy,

I am Rhonda Winfield, mother of LCPL Jason C. Redifer, USMC, who bravely and proudly gave his life for this country on January 31, 2005. I am still very much in the raw stages of my grief and have been extremely affected by the message you are sending out to our fellow Americans, as well as the rest of the world. I have watched, day by day, as you have continued to camp outside of our President's home in Crawford, Texas. I have listened to you explain to the media that you are the moral voice of America because yours is one of a mother who has lost a child. You present yourself as the true voice of those who have paid the most significant price of war and indicated that you are the spokeswoman for the broken souls of all grieving mothers. You were not, however, the recipient of the next of kin notice delivered to my household and while we perhaps share many emotions at this time, you do not speak for me.

127

While I defend a democratic system that allows our citizens to freely speak our minds, question our leaders when we disagree with their representation and hold those same individuals accountable for the decisions they make, I feel you have crossed the line. The final moment of tolerance came when you participated in erecting a display of crosses bearing the names of each felled service member whose lives have been given in Iraq to pay the price for such a freedom. You exercise the rights, which they have purchased for you, only to disrespect and degrade what they held high enough to die for and what you value so little as to exploit. While casualty numbers are facts, you have crossed a moral boundary in using the name of my son, as well as many others, to promote an agenda that he would be no part of. It is more than enough that his life was given to continue your ability to do just that very thing, if as an American you saw fit to do so. Must you further the pain of that fact for our family by soliciting his sacrifice for your purpose. He believed in nothing you stand for and it saddens my heart beyond words to know that he is, in death, being used as a pawn to empower your message.

My son was only 19 years old but knew what a precious gift freedom was and valued it enough to lay his young life down for that very thing. He volunteered for his duty knowing that there is always a human cost of war. He also was wise enough to understand that there would ultimately be a far greater human cost to avoiding this war. Let me remind you that Americans were attacked on our soil. Innocent countrymen whose only crimes were going about their daily lives were murdered that September morning and the evil forces that orchestrated and supported those horrific events, as well as the others that yet await us, must not be allowed to prevail. Jason knew that these terrorists must be engaged on their soil before we were forced to defend ourselves against them again on our own. He valiantly served to keep this from the doorsteps of our children.

We may not agree on the reasons that we are engaged in Iraq but we are there fighting nonetheless. Anti-American sentiment cannot be perpetuated by insisting on the rapid withdrawal of our troops from Iraq. The *message that would be sent to the entire globe would have ramifications of a magnitude too severe for us to even comprehend as we sit here in our free, comfortable homes pontificating the current state of things. American troops have a job to finish there and they must remain until they do.*

Cindy, I have spent many hours with the survivors of the incident that took my son, as well as many other brave young men whom I've met while visiting Bethesda Naval Hospital and Walter Reed Army Medical Center. I have watched the tears roll down their faces as they have watched the coverage of events that they have lived depicted in the media. My son's unit fought for six months in the "triangle of death," just south of Baghdad. Nine days before they were to return home, and on the final patrol of their mission, they were killed by an IED. The only two survivors of this brutal attack were not even aware of the details for weeks. They awakened after many surgeries and difficult medical procedures to be informed that they were the only survivors. They were obviously unable to even attend the funerals of the three men that had become such an important part of their lives. They remain hospitalized to this day. They will not only struggle with their physical disabilities but the emotional demons that will haunt them for the rest of their days. They do not understand why their lives were spared when their brothers were taken. They know only one thing for certain. They know this is not something that can ever be allowed to come to our streets. Please don't cheapen that degree of sacrifice, patriotism and selflessness by insinuating to America that you speak for us.

Without dispute, our sons were part of the price paid for our freedom to speak our minds. We both honor them by exercising those rights. Let's make sure we further honor them by speaking a message they would be proud of. We don't have to agree to be right in doing so. We all want our nation's children removed safely from harm's way. Let us unite in encouraging America to pray for a speedy victory, not a rapid withdrawal. Let us together remind our country that we are the Land of the Free, Because of the Brave and let us strive to remember that we are "one nation, under God." Freedom is never free.

As it is said, "For those who have fought for it, Freedom has a flavor the protected will never know." Jason and Casey know.

I am sincerely,
Rhonda L Winfield

I went to bed that night feeling pleased with my letter and anxious for an opportunity to present "the other side of the coin." Be careful what you wish for.

I had decided that I would simply read my letter aloud at the rally and maybe I would even find out how I could get it to Cindy.

When I awakened the next morning I received a phone call from Lynn. Thinking it was just another call to fine tune details for the rally, I greeted her with my usual jokes and immediately noticed that she wasn't laughing. Certain that it was not because my humor was fading, I asked what was up and she said, "I hope you were serious about wanting to get your message out. FOX News just called. They picked up our press release for the Rally in the Valley. They want you to appear on their FOX News Sunday show." After establishing that she was actually not pulling my leg, I took the information that they had left with her. Before I could gather my swirling thoughts, the phone rang again. FOX News was now calling me. They wanted to know if I would consider appearing on the Chris Wallace show the Sunday immediately following the rally. They understood that I had committed to doing the rally and that they would send a car for me when it was over. They told me that I would be put up in the George Hotel and returned home immediately after the live show aired. I was told that my driver would be happy to take me to Arlington to visit Jason's grave on the way home if I chose to do so.

The show was hoping to have two mothers of opposing opinions that had lost children in the war in Iraq. They said they were trying to get someone from the Cindy Sheehan camp and asked if I would mind. MIND! Hello! I was on fire! I assured them that my message would be the same no matter who else joined the program and that I welcomed someone from her camp, if not Cindy herself.

The details were covered and arrangements made and fifteen minutes later I was left alone in the quiet of my house to contemplate my appearance on a national news program–all because I had gotten pissed off at the evening news! What would I wear? What would I say? It all seemed just a little too surreal, so I just decided to wing it all. My message was all in my heart. All I had to do was open it.

For the rally I had originally intended to address the crowd, read my letter to Cindy, and then go home. Somehow on the drive to the courthouse I decided that I wanted more than that. I didn't want to stand before these people and just read a letter. They were coming to hear me, as the mother of Lance Corporal Jason Redifer, one of their own who had fallen defending them and while I may convey the same message as the one I had written, they at least deserved to hear it from my heart. I closed my eyes in the car to try to clear my mind and I just decided to go with the newly developed Rhonda Winfield method of public speaking; winging it. That was what all of this was about anyway. It wasn't about a letter or a woman protesting in Texas. It wasn't just about a war in Iraq or who was in the White House. This was about Jason, his sacrifice and the countless other men and women who were living on the edge of death every day for our freedom. I didn't need notes to talk about that.

The rain was sheeting down and those faithful that gathered were drenched. I took the podium on cue and thanked everyone for coming on such a dreary, rainy, wet day and declared that a little rain didn't slow true patriots down. I reminded everyone that it was a hundred and twenty-seven degrees in the sands of Iraq and our men and women there weren't letting it slow them down. I told those that didn't know me that my son, Jason, had died January 31st in Iraq just following the elections there. I told them that he had lived long enough to know that they had been deemed a success. I told them about being able to watch the State of the Union Address following his burial in Arlington and what it meant to me to see the ink on the Iraqi woman's finger.

I reminded them that we had all known since Sunday School that "greater love hath no man than to lay down his life for a friend" and that our children were laying their lives down for people they had never even dreamed of meeting. I told them to look into their own hearts and think about what it must be like to step forward out of your own life and to lay down and completely surrender your life, in the hopes of possibly making some difference in the world. I told them that the 1st Battalion, 2nd Marines of Camp LeJeune, North Carolina had gone forth and done exactly that.

I recounted the last time I had seen Jason and talked of how we had thought of him every minute of every day and how we had sent countless care packages from home. I talked of how he received similar packages from people he had never even met and what that meant to him and his fellow Marines. I told them how he would tell us in letters and phone calls about how much even the least little bit of encouragement from home meant.

I talked a little about understanding the grieving heart and the emptiness that could never be filled that those of us, like Cindy Sheehan, had experienced in losing a child. I explained that I believed that the answers that I thought she was seeking, however, would not come from the President or the media. I thought the answers would have to come from other mothers such as myself who knew our sons can not have gone there and died in vain.

I proclaimed that on September 11th, we were attacked and our innocent citizens were murdered when those Twin Towers fell. We knew we could either sit back and wait for the next attack or we could move forward and stop it now! I reminded them that this was a battle to be waged in their land before it came back to ours and that Jason believed in his President when he told us that.

I reminded everyone that whether or not they believed in the same causes that I did, our troops were in Iraq. We would now simply have two choices. We could wage on until we had victory to continue our freedom and bring freedom to those who have never even dreamt of it or we could come home, surrender and wait. I told them that it

132

was my belief that we could not leave until the job was done.

Most importantly, I told them that as a nation, in spite of our many varied differences, we must come together. Those differences are an amazing thing to be celebrated and that it is what makes us unique.

We had to unite, however, to make sure that those men and women who did come forward and who have given their lives, as well as those who continue to risk their lives every day for our freedom, don't get the message that there is a dissention in the ranks here at home. We must never give them the impression that we are a country divided and that what they are there fighting for is not appreciated or understood here at home.

There were, of course, other speakers and presenters and the whole event had been beautifully arranged and orchestrated. Lynn sure knows how to throw a party! The banners and American flags and patriotic music were a thing of beauty.

The event was finished with a young man with bagpipes. He walked over to me just before he was announced and told me that on this day he would play for Jason.

He stepped forward that day in the rain and played the Marine Corps Hymn and Amazing Grace. As the tears dripped from my eyes I stared straight ahead at a gentleman from the Marine Corps League who showed up in his uniform and had stood at parade rest for the entirety of the program. He was standing there now with both tears and raindrops flowing down his cheeks. That was for my Jason as well. That was for every man and woman who had ever put on a uniform and stepped forward to serve. That was for our country.

I was going home to pick up my suitcase and leave for Washington D.C. I had a voice that needed to be heard. I had a message to take to the world. I was going to hear those bagpipes and see that Marine all the way to our nation's capitol.

CHAPTER 13

FOX SUNDAY

I kissed my children and husband goodbye and climbed into the car that would take me to Washington D.C. I had asked Lynn to accompany me since Scott was unable to go and we picked her up on the way.

Our driver's name was Ty and he did his best to insure that we were comfortable and happy. I had never been "sent for" before and was very intrigued with it all. I chatted him up all the way to D.C. (about 3 1/2 hours away) and would have been much more comfortable sitting up front with him had Lynn not been able to come along.

He left us at the George Hotel and we found our room and settled in. I thought the safe was a microwave and ended up very pleased that I had not tried to pop corn.

We had a lovely dinner at a nearby restaurant and it was wonderful to just get to relax and have girl talk. We had absolutely nothing that we had to do until the following morning and it was nice to have a chance to catch my breath.

We talked about the rally and Lynn listened as I opened up and spilled all of my emotion from the last several days. She listened as I recounted my perhaps not so abridged life history and she listened as I talked intimately and frankly for one of the first times about losing my son. Ironically enough, we barely spoke of the adventure we would be embarking on the following morning.

Maybe it was just too surreal. Maybe it was just too overwhelming to grasp. Maybe I was just too tired.

I climbed into a most comfortable bed and wrapped Jason's robe tightly around me. I had grabbed his bathrobe the night he died and held it to me, smelling the last scent of him on it. I have slept with it every night since. I also snatched a silly stuffed monkey off his bed that the children and I had sent him for a birthday laugh. He mailed it home with some special things that he wanted to keep. He sent them ahead so that they hopefully would not get lost or broken. I didn't let that monkey go for weeks. I often still carry it with me in my purse where no one else can see it, but I know it is there. I have held it for every event that I thought might rattle me or bring me to tears. It is filthy and I am like a little child that will not surrender her teddy bear long enough for it to be laundered.

Courtland and Carter know very well the unspoken value of "Mr. Monkey," as we would come to call him. Sometimes they will just pick him up and bring him along for me as we are going out the door.

I squashed Mr. Monkey up under my chin and slept like a baby.

We awakened fresh and anxious and we left early to make sure we had plenty of time. It was a very short walk and we found our way without incident.

As we were led into the Green Room, the feeling that we were really here started to surround me. We were made very comfortable, offered all sorts of breakfast food and beverage and told to just relax. I was making small talk, with the only other person in the room, over a bagel. He was very polite and minutes after he left the room he appeared on the television screen in there. He was a guest on another Sunday morning show. The title that scrolled along beneath his live shot said something about being FOX's anti-terrorism expert. Great, Rhonda! I certainly hoped you impressed him with your cream cheese selection.

Someone instructing me to come into "Hair and Makeup" called me away from my embarrassment. I could have died. I followed along and left Lynn in the sitting area snapping photos of the famous guests who were pictured all around the walls.

I could only receive two channels at my house: NBC and PBS. I had no idea who any of these people were; not even the host whose show I was going to be a guest on. As it turned out, he was in the make up chair when I was seated for hair. We sat side by side for quite a while and neither of us had a clue that we should meet the other.

I was so relaxed that I'm sure the beautiful woman doing my makeup must have thought I was asleep. It felt so wonderful to have all the brushes gently whispering across my face. I didn't care if she put a clown nose on me. It felt great. When I opened my eyes they were beautiful! I couldn't stop staring at myself. She wanted to know if everything looked O.K. and I thought to myself, "did you see me when I came in here?" "Yes, that's great," I said instead and moved over to take the now vacant chair where Mr. Wallace had been sitting. Lynn was popping in and out to get a couple of photos. The hair lady began working with my hair and asked me if I had anything special that I wanted done. "They weren't very specific when they booked my centerfold" I blurted out, this time unable to catch myself. She and the makeup lady laughed and embarrassment flooded over me once again.

Once I was safely back in the sitting area with Lynn, the door opened and another woman came in pulling a suitcase behind her. I somehow knew that this was the woman who would be appearing with me. I had been given her name and told that she had lost a son about a year before Jason passed away. He was also serving in Iraq and was nineteen years old. I knew she shared Cindy Sheehan's political views and was a member of some organized peace coalition.

When the woman from FOX called me, she wanted to know what group I was with. "Group?" I asked. "I'm just a mother who lost her son." She indicated that would be just fine.

Looking back, I don't know why I didn't research this woman or try to prepare myself. I wasn't even sure what political group she was backed by, although I knew there was one. I didn't bring notes or an agenda. I brought a girlfriend to share small talk with and a broken heart with a message. I somehow decided that would be enough. She was lovely and dressed in a beautiful suit. I had on a blouse and like always, Jason's dog tags. I knew I had one thing she did not. I had a secret weapon. I had Mr. Monkey. It had been exactly two years before that I had sat on that drill field in Parris Island watching my precious boy become a U.S. Marine. I no longer had my graduate but I did have this ragged reminder of him and today I would pull all of the comfort and strength from it that I could.

Without shame, I carried Mr. Monkey into the studio when we were called and she carried her materials.

We were seated, microphoned and given camera instruction. The studio was a little smaller than I had imagined. I was surprised to find that the view in the background was real.

I kept thinking, here I am about to go on live national television, on a news program, on a channel I didn't even get at my house, with a woman whose views I knew nothing of, without as much as one stupid notation, and I'm concerning myself with the view!

We were told this was to be a discussion and not a debate. I took this to mean that there would be no weapons involved. I guess "The Jerry Springer Show" didn't tape in this building.

I decided that no matter what, I would let her have the last word. If I couldn't be prepared, at least I could be polite. After all, this was my first time out of the box.

"And we're live in 10, 9, 8..."

Oh dear God, that's it! That's all we're going to be told before we begin. Well, O.K. Let me buckle my seat belt.

I only remember seeing a camera for a split second. I never felt the lights. I never felt nervous after "2,1 and GO!" I closed my hand around Mr. Monkey on my lap and was as ready as I had ever been for anything.

The following is an actual transcript from the show:
Transcript: Mothers of Slain Soldiers Debate Iraq War

Monday,

*August
29, 2005*

**FOX
NEWS**

WASHINGTON - The following is a transcript from "FOX News Sunday With Chris Wallace" on August 28, 2005.

CHRIS WALLACE, HOST: *In Crawford, Texas,* **Cindy Sheehan** *(search) led a rally of anti-war demonstrators. She told the crowd their efforts could end the fighting in Iraq. Nearby, supporters of President Bush yelled, "Cindy, go home," and said her actions give hope to the enemy.*

We're joined now by two mothers whose sons, when they were both just 19, were killed in Iraq. They now have very different views about the war that the U.S. is waging. Rhonda Winfield's son, Marine Lance Corporal Jason Redifer, died this January, just one week before his tour was up. Rhonda supports the president's policies.

Barbara Porchia's son, Army Reservist Private First Class Jonathan Cheatham, was killed in July of 2003. She says it's time to start pulling out our troops.

Thank you both for joining us today, and we are very sorry for both of your losses.

BARBARA PORCHIA: *Thank you.*

RHONDA WINFIELD: *Thank you.*

WALLACE: *Let's start with your sons. Both of them enlisted in the service. Barbara, you say that Jonathan died for what he believed to be right. Does that make it tougher now for you to oppose the war?*

PORCHIA: Jonathan died because when we were - we started the war. We were told that there were **weapons of mass construction** (search), imminent threat and connection to 9/11. He joined the military right after 9/11, and he said, "Mom, I want to do something to protect our country."

But as time went on, I looked at the weapons of mass destruction, imminent threat and connection to 9/11. Those things all panned out not to be true. And that is when you look at it and you say what are we really over there for if those things are not true.

WAIIACE: Rhonda, let me turn to you. As the casualties of more American troops mount, as Iraqis haggle over the constitution, no doubts at all about staying the course in Iraq, no doubts at all about more mothers sending more sons and daughters to fight there?

WINFIELD: Absolutely no doubts. And I don't say that because my son is gone and can't come back. I have an older son who is in the Army and is still serving and will possibly go as well. We have to be here. We cannot simply stay here and wait for them to come to our shores. We were attacked. Our citizens were murdered on September 11th, and waiting for the next move was not an option.

WAIIACE: Barbara, let's talk about the other mothers and other sons. Is it fair to them to see folks back home protesting, raising questions about whether it's worth risking their lives?
PORCHIA: The way I look that is all parents - we love our kids. We love our children dearly. And when we send our children off, I think that we should understand what we're sending our children off for.

Since we don't have weapons of mass destruction, imminent threat or connection to 9/11, and our president's now saying that our soldiers are bringing democracy to Iraq and that our soldiers are dying for a noble cause, I wish he could just explain to us what the noble cause is, so as mothers send their children off they could tell their children what they're so proud of them for, you know, doing and explain to them what they're actually over there for.

My thing now is why are we fighting this war? And if we're fighting terrorists, we were fighting terrorists in Iraq - I mean in Afghanistan. So why did we go to Iraq to fight terrorists? Osama bin Laden, which caused 9/11, was in Afghanistan, so why did we choose to go to Iraq?

I think that's a question that I would have and I think a lot of other mothers - and I don't think that we are taking the morale down of the troops, because I think all of our troops understand that we love them and care for them dearly. We just want them, if they have got to be over there, to know what the reason is.

WALLACE: Rhonda, I know that's a big concern of yours, the question of the message - if there's home front protest, the message that sends and, as Barbara brought up, the issue it has on morale. How do you answer her statements?

WINFIELD: I think not only is it devastating to our troops to see, as they go out every day, putting their lives on the line, watching their brothers and sisters fall for what they are so courageously fighting for, to think that there is dissension among the ranks back home.

They need to know that they are fully supported, fully believed in and fully engaged by all of our concerns. I just have to think that - my son carried with him a simple stuffed animal that my younger children sent to him, and he wrote home and told us touching this was home, thinking of us sending this was home.

And he also called and told us about a letter that they received from someone at home, supposedly in support, until they called them all baby killers and murderers. I know what that did to my son that day. And I know when they're there and they hear what's going on here, they can't feel our support.

And not only is it just blatantly an insult to our troops, it says to the whole world that we cannot even unite as a country to defend the liberties that our children are fighting for.

WALLACE: Barbara, how do you respond to Rhonda?

PORCHIA: I think what we're looking at here and what we need to understand - we need to find out what we're fighting for. What are we in Iraq for? You know, like I keep saying, everything that we were told we're going for is not there. So why are we sending our troops there?

And I think as far as supporting our troops, I love my troops. I support them constantly. And for them to think that possibly we have a disagreement here is taking down morale there - I think we need to look at other things that possibly could take down morale.

How do you think morale was felt by the troops when we went into Iraq, and we were told there were weapons of mass destruction, imminent threat and connection to 9/11, and now all of a sudden the administration came out and said we made a mistake? What do you think that did to the morale?

And then, one other question is we were told, as we were sending our troops over there, that they would have the best of equipment and everything to fight with to be able to get this war over with and come home. And then many, many months later we have Donald Rumsfeld coming out and saying, "Oh, we went to war with what we had." I don't that, you know, we're taking the morale of our troops down. I think I support them by saying if we've got to stay there, do what we've got to do and then get them out of there.

WALLACE: Rhonda?

WINFIELD: I have seen pictures of entire fighter jets buried in the sand. I have seen pictures of the entire cache of weapons that just my son's unit would uncover from homes. I have no concerns about there being weapons of mass destruction of some regard there that were going to be used against Americans.

I know we get just what we see from our evening news. I also know that a lot of the good that's going on there is not conveyed and I just think we have to stay the course. I know why my son went there. I know why Barbara's son went there. They watched those towers fall, and they knew that the liberties that we have were something that they believed were worth fighting for. That hasn't changed. And we either *approach them on their soil or we sit here idly and wait for them to come to ours.*

WALLACE: Let me ask you about that, about the threat. The president went out this week to try to rally support, perhaps in response to Cindy Sheehan and the anti-war movement getting so much attention, and one of the points he made is that if we pull out now that it sends a terrible signal of weakness around the world. Let's take a look to what the president had to say about that.

(BEGIN VIDEO CLIP)

GEORGE W. BUSH, PRESIDENT OF THE UNITED STATES: An immediate withdrawal of our troops in Iraq or the broader Middle East, as some have called for, would only embolden the terrorists.

(END VIDEO CLIP)

WALLACE: Barbara, let's talk about that. Let's talk about what would happen if you had your way. If we pull out our troops either right away or begin to pull them out - but that's what you want, is to get the troops out of there - what do you think happens to Iraq, and what do you think happens to the war on terror?

PORCHIA: I think we have to first look at 9/11. There was no connection to 9/11 in Iraq, OK? And I think that we were fighting very strongly in Afghanistan to deal with terrorism. And I think that if we had focused in Afghanistan and stayed the course in Afghanistan, we today would not be sitting here discussing about trying to pull our troops out of Iraq.

WALLACE: I know, but for good or ill, we're in there now. We have 139,000, 140,000 troops there. What do you think happens to Iraq, what do you think happens to the war on terror, if now we pull the troops out?

PORCHIA: You know, I don't think that we can say what will happen if we leave our troops there. But right now they're debating over the constitution while our soldiers are still fighting and dying. And if we pull out - if we stay there, is there a guarantee that everything will be fine? No, there's not.

And if we pull out, you know, like I say, there is no guarantee there as well. But I'm looking at what is the reason for our troops dying. And we need to look at that and say if our troops are dying for a noble cause, our president needs to come out and tell us what the noble cause is. If we don't know what the noble cause is and there really is no true noble cause, why are we keeping our troops there? I say pull them out.

WALLACE: Let me turn to you, Rhonda. If we do stay the course, how long are we going to have troops there, and what can we say that we are going to accomplish?

WINFIELD: I think it's absolutely unfair to tie anyone's hands and force them to give us a definite time line. I think we just have to keep the end result in mind. The Iraqi people deserve to be free. Our country deserves to have our freedoms defended. We have continued to make progress.

In response to Afghanistan, there are terrorists gladly claiming every day responsibility for the attacks on our troops. Obviously, we're in a place that we need to be. I just don't think we can give a definite time line. I'm sure all of us pray that it could be today that it would be over and there would be no one else to have to lose their life. But there is a human cost to war. And in this situation, there will be an even greater human cost to not being at war.

WALLACE: We have a little bit of time left. Rhonda and Barbara, for all your differences, there's obviously a great

Page 4 of 4

deal that binds you as two mothers who have shared a terrible loss that thankfully none of us can even imagine. What would you like to say to each other? What would you like us to understand?

WINFIELD: Well, I think we had a little time to talk before the show, and you don't even have to say anything. You hug one another and you know that the hole in your heart that never is repaired is only felt by someone else who has a like hole. And we have a kinship, as do all of the other parents and family members who have lost ones, that no one else will understand.

WALLACE: Barbara?

PORCHIA: I look at Rhonda and we both understand, like she says, that there is a relationship between us, because we've both lost our sons there. And what I would like to think of is that when I look at other mothers, I don't want to see other mothers have to go through what I go through every day.

WINFIELD: Absolutely.

PORCHIA: And I support those troops, but I support them in saying if they're in harm's way for reasons that cannot be explained, I say pull them out and get them out. As far as looking at the whole scenario, I think that we have to look at death as an equalizer. Once we're dead, there is nothing else there. And we need to think about are we really playing politics with our soldiers over there, or are they there for all the right reasons.

WALLACE: Well, we have to leave it there. Rhonda and Barbara, J want to thank you both so much for joining us today to share your thoughts about the war. And from all of us, thank you for your sons' service to our country.

We honor their memory.

We arrived back on the steps of the hotel with a little time to spare.

"Mrs. Winfield," I heard someone yell. I turned to see Ty, our driver from the previous day. He was going to be driving us home as well. He congratulated me on the program and began to load us up.

We took the scenic route out of Washington and at one point Ty called my attention out the window. "Look over there" he said. "That's a reminder of what you're fighting for." I looked out of my window to see the White House.

We arrived at Arlington National Cemetery and I gave Ty directions to find Jason's grave. I asked Lynn to go with me. She felt like she was intruding on something very personal and sacred to me. I wanted her to go to the place that marked this life. She obliged and we walked toward his stone.

I could see a couple in the general area that we were heading toward. As we came closer the woman knelt down over a stone and began to weep. I soon saw that she was grieving at the stone directly beside Jason's.

I knew immediately that this woman was a mother. I never considered she could be anyone else. I don't know what it is exactly that gives us away. Maybe we just slump a little further over the head stone. Perhaps we are just a little more bent. Maybe we are even just a little more broken. Maybe, as mothers, we can sense emptiness in each other's arms that could only come from having a child ripped away. I'm sure I will never be able to define it, but I recognized it in that woman that day.

I stood beside her and put my hand on her shoulder. Like Lynn, I didn't want to intrude on her sorrow, but I wanted to reach out to her. She looked up at me in surprise.

"Is this your son?" I whispered.

"Yes," she answered quietly.

"This is my son" I replied and waved my hand toward Jason's marker.

She stood up and I embraced her. We held onto one another like two souls on a sinking ship. I suppose at that moment that is exactly what we were. I knew so much more about this woman. I had felt her heart. I had felt her life break. I had felt her soul crumble. I stood with her now, side by side, as we looked over two plain marble stones that read our children's names.

There was nothing more to be said.

I don't know which one of us left first. I don't recall even being aware of her existence after that moment. I became lost in my thoughts of Jason.

Every visit I had ever made here was basically the same. I would want to hurl myself onto the ground and sob until I could stand it no more. I wanted to just melt into the sod and disappear. I would leave from every visit, feeling again like I had left my son alone in that field.

Today, I was filled with questions. Had I done what Jason would have been proud of? Had I represented his thoughts and ideals in a way that would do them justice? Was it futile to have even come? Should I have stayed at home and waited on Justin to need me?

All of these questions raced through my mind briefly and then the few tears that came that day seemed to spill in order to flush them away.

I was engulfed by a sense of peace that I had never experienced there. I just stood there and let it wash over me.

I looked at Lynn and announced that I was ready to go. I was ready to take my leave.

We returned to the car and began our journey home. I knew then that I had come because I was supposed to and I had done what I had been sent to do.

I left Arlington that day and didn't look back.

I wish my future trips would have been able to fill me with the same peace and that I would never again have had to experience that betrayal that always seemed to leave with me. But, I had one special day. One day, I was given a gift and my questions were answered. My doubts were relieved and I left knowing that Jason was coming too.

CHAPTER 14

A LONG WAY DOWN

The days following all the August excitement left me struggling to keep my head above water. Every single day found me wearily forcing myself out of bed to go to work or staying in my bed if I could avoid going to work. I would save all of my energy, emotional and physical for the activities that I would be required to engage in. I did everything I could to try to be "normal" for Courtland and Carter but along with losing their brother they were losing their mother too. I could barely stand the thought of driving the two hours required to go visit Justin and Missy even though I missed them greatly.

They were expecting their first child around the end of January, 2006. The news had been absolute music to my ears. I knew immediately that Justin had just been given direction and a purpose far greater than any he had ever known and his life would be changed instantly because of it. They were so excited and a new kind of love and admiration settled over them and with it came healing for them both. I wanted to shower them with love and attention and could not summon the energy to do so. I spent as much time with them as I could and it took absolutely everything out of me. I was determined not to let this amazing miracle leave me behind so I kept pushing forward.

So much loss and grief over the past year. It struck me that the baby's birth date was scheduled to be so close to the anniversary of Jason's death on the 31st of January. I believe that this served as a reminder that the God who has taken is the same God who has given. I think this glimpse of light for us was significant.

I was absolutely exhausted with life and honestly thought that I was dying from grief. I literally believed that it was taking my life.

My marriage had experienced everything from basic survival because we refused to let failure be an option, to a level of connection that was almost celestial. It was just as the grief pendulum was. It would swing the entire range, with no expectation of where tomorrow would take you. Scott was patient and faithful. We just seemed to know who was expected to carry the love on any given day and would step to the plate as necessary. He had so much to be responsible for. He was forced to completely take care of our lives while I could not handle my own. This was so ironic. As many wives, I often seemed to think that there was very little that he could do right without my direction and yet now, in my most desperate state, I was just so grateful for his dedication to trying.

We worked so hard at discovering who this new couple was. We seemed to have left behind the people we had been and began to blossom into people we had never met. We had shared something that in many ways had truly made us one unit. Of course, this realization was often tarnished when I had visions of dragging him behind the car because he forgot to pick up milk. He had been a dairy farmer for crying out loud! How far from his mind could it have been at any one moment! What could he have possibly been thinking about, aside from running our entire household and anticipating my imminent breakdown? Oh, did I mention dealing with my slight mood bounce?

I think if you asked him today, Scott would tell you that he knew I was still in there all along. He says that the minute the Marines left and he saw me throw myself headlong into the mechanics required of the situation, that he knew we would ultimately be O.K. He had often thought about this day and knew that if it had ever come to our house that I would, in fact, cease to exist at that very moment and would never be found again. I don't know what caused Scott to glimpse a future for either of us when it actually happened, but I am sure glad he did. His belief in it must have been mighty powerful. His belief in me must have been as well.

Grief is such a tool of Satan for many reasons but is especially effective in the dissolution of relationships. No one person is at the same place in their grief for any set amount of time and healing is often one step forward and two steps back. Two people experiencing the same kind of grief are never going to be experiencing the swings in syncopation. Therefore, as a couple you will never be where your mate is. I have found this a curse. I have found this a blessing.

I had been forced to also redefine my relationship with my oldest son. I had to try to figure out what he was needing in a mother now and somehow summon the strength to offer it. He was no longer a child and was embarking on the great adventure of having a child himself.

Courtland was becoming such a young man. He had to step right over so much of his childhood during our family's year of crisis. I would see him being my protector and would listen to a wisdom in him that was far beyond his little years. I know well the angel who walks with him.

Carter was his own unique little self and I could see so much of Jason's innocence and silliness in him. He has such purity of heart and love of his family.

They are all such tremendous people and I was sinking in my inability to be worthy of them. I knew Jason would not be able to bear seeing me suffer at all and certainly not to the point that I couldn't give my all to his brothers whom he loved so dearly.

I kept fighting. It seemed the harder I tried, the lower I fell. I refused to let anyone on the outside see me crumbling. I know those closest to me knew and felt powerless to help me but those on the outskirts remained impressed with my strength and ability.

I wonder what they would have thought if they could have seen me behind the doors of my prison. I had been attending a grief group on Monday nights and found it a sanctuary. I immediately became connected to the others there but was far too upset by their loses to really focus on the work needing to be done with my own.

It was so unnatural for me to open myself up that way. I immediately fell into my pattern of focusing on someone else. I amazed them for a while at my ability to come to group so soon after Jason's death and to be so composed. Quickly, however, they began to realize that I was either letting it all loose somewhere else or was building myself up for an emotional explosion. Unfortunately, the latter seemed to be imminent. I just kept spiraling downward. The energy needed to just maintain was so much more than I had. Our leader, Barb Swett, could see through me and I knew it. God had sent her to me. I knew it because I had no other explanation for why I answered her invitation to this group in the first place. She kept reaching out for me but I would not grab the lifeline.

I prayed so hard for rescue. I pleaded with God to either save me or take me but to let me escape from this purgatory from which I seemed doomed.

During these months, there had been so many services and events and dedications and celebrations. I felt like I was just living from event to event. Each one took so much emotionally that it seemed like I would only start to catch my breath before the next one came along. I was always so honored to have Jason remembered that I threw myself into every one. I put on the face, made sure to smile and always managed at least a few sincere words of appreciation. I would NEVER let myself just surrender to the emotion that any of these days elicited. God forbid that people should see me cry during a forum revolving around the loss of my child. I felt I owed it to them to be able to express my gratitude in some sort of respectable manner that didn't involve making them squirm with discomfort in their seats. Watching someone slip from the curb of stability is not a pretty sight. Certainly not what people are expecting when they invite you out for a buffet dinner, a Ruritan meeting and a plaque.

Everyone wanted so desperately to show respect for Jason's service and to memorialize the goodness that he held in his heart. They all felt the pain that radiated from us and while each and every one wanted desperately to give us some sort of healing, there was nothing to do for us but be our friends. I owed it to all of these people to attempt to show them how much we appreciated their love. Unfortunately, killing myself in the process was not the best tack. Their gestures were overwhelming and the stamina required to sustain the level of behavior I had deemed appropriate was overwhelming as well.

I had saved everything I could get my hands on that involved Jason and chronicled it all in albums that I kept in his room. It was not like a shrine exactly. We didn't revere it as a holy type place but rather as a place of comfort where we could go hang out in Jason's ridiculous yard sale chair and absorb ourselves in his stuff. It was as close as we could be to the tangible Jason.

I had a reporter ask me not too long ago what it was that broke me down when I thought of or talked about Jason. Without a doubt it is Jason in the tangible sense. When I think of never touching him, smelling him, and hearing him again. I look around at all of these amazing pictures that we have and I'm so grateful for each of them. Then, I wonder how I will ever remember his voice? It was this concern that would always take me down. I couldn't bear the thought of never hearing him call up the stairs to me at the end of the night again. I would just sit in that room for hours, trying to hear his voice in my head so it wouldn't slip away.

I was sinking lower and lower. I couldn't hear Jason's voice. I couldn't find mine.

Barb finally called me out one night at grief group. She was tired of watching me work so hard bottling up my pain and I was given an assignment that night. I had just been curled up there in my chair listening to everyone else when she spoke to me and asked me if I took time to journal. I had been a big fan of journalizing my entire life but knew I had not done so for quite some time. I was given an assignment and told to return with it the next week. I expected to flow through it with some entry flowery enough for pride and prejudice and went straight home to find my last journal. When I found it, I discovered that my last entry was the day that Jason left for Iraq. I guess I didn't need to journal after that because I wrote him every single day. Then, since his death, I had thought about it many times but felt like I didn't have the emotional energy to participate in the process of letting it all out. I knew that once my mind started letting it all go, my pen would never be able to keep up.

I decided to sit at my computer because I could type faster than I could write and as I began, something rolled over me. When I started, I couldn't stop. It was not Jane Austin pouring forth. It was I. Like I had never acknowledged. I wrote and wrote and wrote. It was ugly and bitter and frightening. I talked of anger and pain and fear and of wanting to die. I said every horrible and evil thought that had crossed my mind since January and I couldn't stop it. It flowed from me like a river with no end. I was a woman possessed! I not only poured forth my deepest pain and feelings but I spouted off about others as well. I damned the people that expected you to be "over it" within 72 hours following interment and those that I ended up feeling responsible for because they "couldn't handle it." I said that I was tired of trying to make others around me always feel better and sick of comforting them when they came to comfort me. I had actually been given a gift basket from my friend, Keedie, which held items for these people. The card stated "to comfort those who come to comfort you." She knew how the cycle worked and told me she would be back later for the things that I would actually need for me.

I claimed that I was fed up with the people in this world that constantly get a pass for bad behavior just because it had always been their pattern in the past. "Oh, well, that's just so-and-so." No more from me! That's just so-and-so because that is how so-and-so has been allowed to behave.

I cursed the people, family members especially, who took advantage of the people who were grieving the hardest.

I blasted the people that I had tried to make comfortable because they just didn't know how to handle the "new me." I refused to work at making them understand any further that I am not the same person. People tell you not to hold it in, in fact criticize you because you seem too composed and then absolutely freak when you lose it! Then, of course, you are mentally unbalanced and are certainly not dealing with the death appropriately.

I hated friends and relatives that all said, "Call us if you need anything" and then suddenly aren't available for lunch, an outing, or even a phone call. So many people believe that if they bake you a casserole and write you a card that they have fulfilled the "friend of the grieving" requirement and can go home and sleep, guilt-free. They can then be sure to avoid any gossip that would have happened in their absence and can tell others how they were there for you.

What kind of a person knows you your whole life and then vanishes from the face of the Earth as soon as their check clears the florist?

It is somehow a faux pas of Miss Manner's magnitude to go out of your house until you can wear a lampshade on your head for the party. Yet, if you wear the damn lampshade and sing "Beer Barrel Polka" then you obviously need serious therapy to get in touch with your suppressed feelings.

I was never again going to answer the phone to speak to those that only called to dump on me. If, by some fluke of nature I was having a decent day, they could smell it on the air and would call to torpedo it by expressing their inability to venture on in life due to the grief they had been burdened with during this ordeal. They would simply whine the same things every single conversation. Yes, damn it! We ALL missed him terribly! We ALL wanted him back! We ALL thought he was special! Blah, blah, blah, blah, blah! I get it!!! Now, you get this– SHUT UP!

What kind of a person calls you to see how you are doing and then before you even have a chance to lie and pretend to be making it, has launched into a dissertation about how life has wronged them! Forty-five minutes later and you have yet to utter a word!

I was sick of going to work every day in tears. I was sick of dealing with the guilt of watching my husband feed my children, bathe my children, take them to school, pick them up from school, take them to sports practices and games and be both father and mother to them. He was laundry, he was dishes, he was cleaning, he was OVERWHELMED! He would never say it. He was doing an amazing job at it all and I couldn't stand how horrible it made me feel and I was too powerless to do anything about it but cry!

I was angry that losing one son kept me from being a mother to the other three! Everyone related to me, that they not only lost Jason, they lost me as well! I was tired of trying to make my way back. I hated having to work so hard to be something for everyone else! I was just trying to live!

I HATED myself for not having anything left to offer my husband! He was grieving, he was lost, he needed me more than ever and all he was getting was the responsibilities that I couldn't handle! Still, he loved me and lined up every morning to see what bone he might get thrown that day! I couldn't watch it any longer and I was seemingly unable to change it!

I HATED GOD for leaving me like this! Is it not enough that he took my son? Could he not just leave me with enough strength to take care of my remaining family? Fine! Leave me a basket case forever but PLEASE don't make them suffer anymore!

I was in a rant and I let out all of the rage that had been boiling up inside of me for months. I wrote and I wrote and I wrote. When I was finished, I was truly finished. I had found the key. I had unlocked the misery and was finally headed toward freedom.

I took the "journal" the following week and scared the Hell out of everybody in the room as I read it out loud. I read all of it without stopping, knowing that if I did I might not get through it. It wasn't enough to just write it and release it from my heart. I had to put it out there for others to see. I had to show how ugly and raw and broken I was to those who would understand like no one else. Why had I been so afraid to go against what I had always known and let these dear souls help me? They were the safest place for me to lay it all down and yet I had kept it in.

Well, it was certainly out there now. When I finished reading and looked up at their faces, they were pale. I believe shocked may be more appropriate. I didn't care. It felt liberating. I knew I looked like a junkie who had hit rock bottom. I was emotionally spent but at least I was headed for detox. I knew I had a problem, I had admitted it, claimed it, and was now ready to cure it. I had a long way to go but I was mentally clean and sober and would never be strung out on grief again.

I started to put my clothes on even on days I had nowhere to go. I forced myself to get groceries and I suddenly started to find the joy in cooking again. I committed two days to nothing but laundry and was able to save my family from becoming nudists. My little group cheered each accomplishment! They knew how significant even these baby steps were. They saw me changing. They saw me starting to show real joy at times and knew it was honest.

I began a nutrition program with vitamins and supplements and started dropping weight. I wanted to move again and so I did. I had wrestled with my weight since I was twenty-five years old. I did the "yo-yo" with the best of them. Up, down. Up more. Once Jason left for Iraq, I totally began self-destruction. No one understood why I was behaving in such an extreme way. They didn't know yet that he wasn't coming back. I knew that if he made it home, he would be mortified to see me. His heart would have been broken by my sad physical shape. He would see how I had suffered. I wished I could lose it before he would see me again. I think now I will.

Once we had gotten the news, it was all downhill from there. My health had declined so much that I truly expected to die, if not from a broken heart then from one that was suffocated by fat.

Now, I was changing. I was becoming leaner and more fit. I could feel the vitamins working in my body. My engine was finally getting a tune up. I had just about been ready for the junkyard and now I was on my way to becoming a high performance machine!

I received a satellite radio system for my birthday and started cranking big hair bands in my car all day on my mail route. I delivered letters while screaming "Panama" at the top of my lungs. Sadly, people have come to expect far less from postal employees, so it was not a problem.

I unloaded my burden, faced some demons and rose up from the ashes of my death in the front yard. I am not the same. I never will be. I am learning who this new person is. I have decided one thing for certain. I am going to surrender this new chick completely to God. He answered my prayers. He didn't answer them like I asked him to, He answered them in the way I needed him to. He broke me. He let me fall until I slammed the bottom and it was only then that I would truly surrender. He would not take me. He made me stay and made me find something within myself. When I found it, He started to pull me up. I don't know what He has planned for me but I am going to strive to live every day trying to stay open to being led in the direction to do His will. I have always had a belief. I felt like it grew with every year of my life that passed. I would have told you that I was basically right with the Lord. I certainly didn't want to go around acting like Rhonda, The Super Christian, but I thought He and I had an understanding.

That may have been true, but through the most unimaginable torture of my life, I have now found the blessing. How can you feel blessed when you have had to bear the death of your son? Because the One who knows what it is like to give His Son for me, showed me the way. He would not let me die, for that was the path that Satan had for me. He knew that living would be harder but He has a plan and will continue to give me these little blessings as consolation prizes for staying in the game.

CHAPTER 15

THE VISITATION

On October 18, 2005, I was slowly beginning to emerge from the nighttime fog that had been my slumber when I was jolted to consciousness by a news mention on the radio. I was thrown backward in time nine months to the morning when I felt the stab of hearing Jason's name actually announced as a news item. I'll never forget how hearing someone read his precious name could pierce my heart and leave me sweating. It was undeniably real at that moment. The world was being put on notice.

Our radio is set to an AM station that we can barely, at best, pick up. We awaken to a morning farm show daily and I know I've overslept when I start singing in my mind along with the jingle that reminds us to "just add cottonseed" to our cattle's feed. Shortly before this ditty, however, we are treated to the day's news headlines, the birthday list for local residents and finally a reading of the daily "pearl of wisdom" which will have been sent in by a listener. On February 1, 2005 as I numbly prepared myself for the above list, I was shattered to hear the name of my precious child identified as the Marine killed from the Valley yesterday.

On this particular morning in October, as I struggled to coerce my legs to the floor, I heard what I thought to be "the Second Valley Marine to be killed in the war in Iraq." I raced to the television while yelling at my husband to see if he had heard anything else. He had caught only what I had and neither of us could find out anything further until much later in the day. When our local television news aired nothing to even tease us with, I began to pray that my mind had played tricks on me and that perhaps this was untrue. Sadly, our local evening news broke with the lead story that a Marine whose home was only about fifteen miles from mine had died due to small arms fire in Iraq. He too was nineteen years old and was killed just one day before his twentieth birthday. I saw his younger brother, Justin, speak so well to the television camera as he told our community that he knew that Daniel was now one of the Marines "guarding the gates of Heaven." So many emotions flooded over me. Lance Corporal Daniel Bubb, 19 years old, from Grottoes, Virginia had died but a baby, just as Jason had. He had a brother named Justin, just as Jason had. Justin was one of two younger brothers at home, just as Jason had two left behind. Daniel's mother was obviously a young mother as well and I knew immediately what that meant in terms of loss for her. For young Justin to have made the remarks that he made so soon after the news of his family's horrible loss and to have put it in such context, assured me that this was the brother of someone who knew his mind and believed in his whole heart in what he was doing by becoming a Marine. It becomes infectious and filtrates throughout your entire family and circle of friends until they all become the believers too. This was obviously a young man who believed in what his brother stood for and was immediately able to find some comfort in that.

I hung on every word and immediately tried to look up the family in the phone book. There was only one listing so I gave it a try. I had no idea what I was going to say but I needed to connect with them somehow. I needed it for myself as much as I thought I needed it for them. An answering machine greeted me in a friendly voice that I knew immediately must have been that of Daniel's mother. It was a voice full of love and life and spoke of a joyful woman who welcomed you to leave a message. I was enormously sad to hear her speak because I could imagine what her broken voice would sound like now that it mimicked what her broken heart was feeling. The announcement didn't assure me that I had the correct home so I preceded my attempt to reach out with, "I certainly hope I have the right number..." and then babbled something that I'm sure was completely inept but hoped would suffice for condolences.

I had so many raw emotions resurfacing inside me. It hadn't seemed as though I had made much progress in my healing process until I felt the sudden contrast with this fresh, raw grief. The thin line that had been created that kept me from teetering over into oblivion was now quivering like a plucked violin string and balance had never been my strong suit. I had suddenly had the horrible hammer of death dropped onto me again and while subsequent wounds never have the same flesh-ripping feel that the first one does on an unadulterated soul, the wound reopens to the same painful, agonizing, bleeding state just the same. I had lost another son. The cannon that shot through my being at the sight of those bringing my next of kin notification had once again lifted me out of my shoes, thrown me in pieces into the wind and dropped me at the doorstep of my own death. I had to go to this family and wrap my arms tightly around Daniel's mother, Janie, and hold on until the Angel of Death had passed over us both.

I didn't have to wait long for a response to my message. I had reached the correct household and Daniel's mother and stepfather returned my call quickly. I had hoped that they were screening their calls, if for no other reason than to try to filter the avalanche of media attention that they were already receiving. I was completely unprepared for what they had to say to me.

They were beyond kind. They were appreciative to a point that overwhelmed me. They were reaching out for a lifeline and were desperately hoping I could be it. They extended like sympathies to my family and me and assured me that we had been in their daily thoughts and prayers. They had lived their worst fear through me first and were now realizing that it had been a dress rehearsal. We needed each other in the worst way.

It was decided when we would meet and I felt as though I was counting the minutes. I prayed for God to impart some words of wisdom on me that I could pass along. I had nothing but a heart full of both good intentions and selfish need.

I spoke with Tammy later that evening to share my experience thus far and ironically discovered that she worked with Daniel's stepfather, Steve. She only knew two people who had served in this war and now both were dead. She and I had never really had the opportunity to grieve the loss of Jason together, even though I knew her loss was great as well. She had come to me immediately, as I knew she would when she heard the devastating news of Jason's death. I could not, however, drop myself into her arms and empty my heart as I so desperately needed to do. To do so would mean a certain confession of truth that I was too fragile to handle. As I pulled away, she picked up her cue and reached out to help fill a void for Justin. He felt a safety in her that allowed him to let her in. She carried him then, as she would continue to do for many months following.

As Tammy and I echoed our pain and grief for the Bubb family, we knew that we would embark on this together. A two-pronged attack, we knew that in reaching out to them we could reach out to each other in a way that we had been unable to do. Through my mask of empathy for this family, I could let my guard down enough to be loved by one of the only people who had loved me unconditionally throughout my adult life.

We met at the Bubb's house the following day. I arrived a few minutes before Tammy and began my journey inside. The garage was filled with "Danielism" everywhere. Banners that had been made to welcome him home from his first tour in Iraq hung over railings. It hurt so much to think of the joy this family had known to receive him home once and then only to have to let go of him again. Now, they would have to let go forever.

I had suffered some incredibly selfish and ugly feelings as I slept the night before and I was so ashamed of them. They lasted only briefly but had branded my heart with their evil. I had heard on the news that Daniel was serving his second tour and I remembered how my family had made banners and signs for Jason's homecoming. I remembered the thrill of finally allowing ourselves to feel the joy of knowing that he would actually be home. At first, I was jealous that this family had been allowed to experience that and to have their son actually step off that bus and run into their arms and give them the sweet kisses that a mother longs for. I was robbed of that and I felt the absence of that moment in my bones. The bitterness quickly turned to pain for them as I thought it through further and imagined having to let Jason leave us once again only to return to harm's way. He would have done so only nine months after his homecoming and suddenly the thought tore me in two. I had an even more horrific jealous pang to take the place of the first when I thought of Daniel's body returning home. I knew that the night before, his family had gone to the funeral home to see him. I was inside out with grief again over not being able to see Jason. I felt so robbed and didn't know how I would ever be able to find true closure, if there is such a thing. I was honestly thankful that the Bubb family would have what I could not, but I was equally envious.

When I awakened the next morning it was with a clarity that had eluded me up to that moment. In my mind's eye I pictured Daniel's parents having to walk into a funeral home and see their child's lifeless body resting eternally in a wooden casket. Until now, I had viewed that thought for myself as an opportunity to touch and embrace what I never would again and had felt so violated that such a small comfort had been stolen from me. Suddenly, I was able to see this as not the gift that I had lost but as the horror of holding your child as a corpse. I watched them as they approached him and felt the pain and indescribable agony that came over them. I knew, at that moment that I had been given a gift, both at the time and again now with my realization. As I thought it through further I came to understand that there is no "better." There is simply "gone." To know that your child will never again walk through your door and light up your soul is to truly know "gone." The details and circumstances that led to the death or the facts and the situation following are inconsequential. There is no "better," there is simply "gone."

I felt the shame of my previous night's thoughts burning on my cheeks as I entered the door of their home. I was greeted by several people and blindly made my way further in. I would know Janie because she would be the broken one. I met both Janie and her sister, Julie, immediately and as we literally fell into one another's arms, I saw that Tammy had entered the room behind me. I tried to fight back my feelings in order to deliver what menial tidbit of comfort I could and while I could feel my mouth open, I have no idea what I said. I somehow seemed able to respond to everything they asked and said and at the time I felt like the foreign language spilling out of me sounded very appropriate. I had no clue who was actually saying it for me, but I was thankful for it. I didn't go much further until I had to come clean. The unworthiness I felt just being in this home after having the thoughts and feelings that I had experienced simply consumed me. Daniel was so alive all around me. He was in photos everywhere and was reflected in the faces of all that gathered to mourn him. His smile burned into my heart. My son. My son, Daniel. I pulled Janie and Julie, close to me and I repented. I told them of the evil that I had let in and I told them of God's merciful gift in the revelation He had given me. They granted me the absolution I needed. The absolution that could come only from them.

I had broken. The dreaded had come and I couldn't fight it back anymore. I saw the tears flowing down Tammy's face and her eyes seemed to plead with me to give into it too. I did. I felt the hot sting of giant, salty drops spill down my face and I knew I had opened the door. Julie wiped my cheek and softly whispered to me, "Do you want to go see him?" I almost hit the floor. I felt the wind rush out of me but I gasped quickly and nodded my head. I could not believe that I had been invited to go along with her for such a sacred journey to the final bed of someone I had never known. Tammy and I took Julie's outstretched hands and began the short walk, ironically, just across the road to the funeral home. It was an incredibly beautiful, warm, sunny day for October and the fresh air felt therapeutic to my lungs. It struck me as odd that Daniel was at the local funeral home because the family church sanctuary was too small to hold even a portion of the people that were expected to come to pay their respects. In our case, the local funeral chapel was too small and we hoped our large church would be adequate.

As we neared the building I actually thought about just letting go and passing out. I was on maximum emotional overload and the combination of grief, fear, empathy and exhaustion was toxic. Tammy's eyes reassured me that we would be O.K. She quietly let me know that this was the moment that I had been denied. I was about to receive an amazing gift and I could either embrace it, change my life, or run from it. She would help me walk forward.

Just inside the funeral home doors, we were greeted by a young associate who seemed strangely too young for the job. He had a beautiful, reassuring and comforting smile that I don't really think you can learn. I was immediately certain that he would have a very bright future in this business. He led us to a small alcove where we were able to view a poignant and beautifully put together video celebrating Daniel's life. There were various still shots of him mingled throughout patriotic pictures of our nation's capitol and lovely music tying it all together. It played on a continuous loop and when we had viewed it all we stood and headed into the room that held his body.

I paused briefly at the door, caught my breath, balled up my latest tissue remnants and said I was ready. Tammy and Julie were on either side of me and I felt as though I was floating toward him. Even from a distance I was struck at how incredibly handsome he was. The family had chosen the same casket for him as I had chosen for Jason. When I reached it, I knew that I belonged here at this moment like I may never have belonged anywhere in my life. I knew this child, this face, and this heart. This was my child, my Marine, my defender of my country's ideals. All that is good in America was laid out in a casket before me. The uniform was crisp and perfect and I reached out to rub his chest. The material was so familiar. I could feel the pride that Jason had for this uniform and I knew Daniel did as well. I believe I have had Jason with me every moment since he died and I had never felt it as strongly as I did in that room. I felt Daniel as well. We were all meant to be there together.

After a long silence, I looked at Julie and asked if I may touch Daniel's beautiful hair. "Of course, he's your son too" was all she said. At that, my heart heaved and the tears came as I have refused to let them before and I reached my hand forward and stroked the soft, baby-fine hairs that formed this handsome and perfect military haircut. Daniel had a cowlick in the front that made me smile beneath my tears and think about how many days he surely stood before a mirror battling with it. All of my children had one somewhere and the vision was so familiar.

I couldn't tell you how long I stood there letting my fingertips brush his cheek and just rubbing his precious head. At one point, I know, I even moved around to the end of the casket so I could get to him even better. I was mesmerized into my own universe where I was oblivious to everything around me. I could only feel Daniel and Jason. They knew what was happening. I was being transformed and forever changed. I kept thanking them both and just took it all in until it had filled all of my senses and a sense of completion came over me.

I had been holding Mr. Monkey and after I came back to reality, Julie asked me about him. I explained and then she took him from my hands and gave him a gentle kiss. Then, she spoke to Daniel and held Mr. Monkey over to give Daniel a kiss on the cheek. She said she could feel the boys smiling on us.

We went back to the family home and said our temporary "good-byes." While I'm sure I was nowhere nearly able to articulate what I had just experienced, I thanked the Bubb family for all that they had given me that day. I went there hoping to find something within myself to give and left with a peace that I had never known. We were everything to each other that day. I know God sent me there and I know God granted me grace. We all knew it was beyond words so we just thanked God for it.

CHAPTER 16

BIRTHDAY AT ARLINGTON

The weekend of November 14, 2005 was packed full of emotion for me since Veterans Day fell on Friday and Jason's twentieth birthday would be on the following Monday. We decided to split the difference and head to Arlington on Sunday. This was the only day that Scott could manage to be away from the farm and I very much wanted him to be able to go with me this time. This would be his first trip back since the burial. He had avoided previous trips by hiding behind farm work but I knew he was not yet able to face the reality of a head stone with his son's name on it.

We decided to make it as much of a celebration as possible. After all, this was a birthday.

As always, the grounds were beautiful. The weather was almost balmy and the sun was shining brightly with only a gentle breeze. The autumn colors and smells were intoxicating. There can be fewer places on Earth more gorgeous than when the fall foliage peaks in our Shenandoah Valley. On this day, however, Arlington National Cemetery came close. The tourists were a little heavier than during some past visits. I assumed this to be because it was Veterans Day weekend.

We entered into the cemetery through the Fort Myer entrance, which always means a security checkpoint and identity check. Again, I felt that sense of pride as I watched these men and women perform their duties in securing their post. Scott's driver's license was checked and held until our vehicle inspection was complete. We were required to turn off our engine and release our hood. Scott answered questions regarding our destination and whether or not we were transporting weapons. The car was then briefly searched, under the hood, in the trunk and underneath with a mirror on a stick. It is always so exciting to me. Finally, we were given the go ahead and we proceeded into the base. We entered the cemetery from the north side and as we approached the main entrance, the children were delighted to see the Lincoln Memorial just across Memorial Bridge. We were waved on through the main intersection due to the pass in our dashboard that we were assigned at Jason's burial. Scott easily found the site, even though this was his first time back. It was a little shocking to see that the row that Jason is in was now complete and another row was almost full. The last time I had been was only about ten weeks before and it seemed there were so many new graves.

Scott parked the car and we unfolded out onto the pavement. I asked Mom to have the children help her get our things in the trunk organized while Scott and I went to the gravesite first. We walked the short distance and stood before the stone that bore the name of our son. I have never been when the sight of this didn't shoot pain straight through me. I remember the first time. It seemed almost more than I could bear. Justin, the boys, my mother and I had all gone for Easter. Only the temporary marker had been up during our previous visit. The head stone wasn't expected for a few more weeks and when I saw it, I almost dropped. I was very pleased after I had a chance to catch my breath that it was there for Easter. It somehow seemed appropriate. Even though I had returned many times since then, it never seemed much easier. I glanced at Scott to see if shock registered in his face. He just looked hollow. I don't think it stunned him in the same way it had me but it was obvious that it hurt him deeply and that he was run over by the truth of it.

We stood in silence. When we finally spoke again it was to convey what it felt like to experience so much agony and not know what to do with it. I told him that every time I came I wanted to lie down on that lush grass in front of his stone and put my face flat down on it and cry. I wanted to just be there, prone and sobbing until I felt I had no more tears left. I knew that below that sod the last of Jason's tangible remains rested. He was with me everywhere I would ever be, yet this is the place where I left what little came home to me. I wanted to run my hands over every blade of grass and scrape my fingernails through the dirt and just be as flat as I could, as close to him as I could be. I had yet to do this for fear of freaking out those that had accompanied me thus far. I knew that perhaps one day soon I would come, alone, and simply allow myself to grieve in just the way my heart was aching to do.

Scott talked about how it still just seemed too impossible to believe. I knew he was thinking about Jason in terms of being dead now. To us, even though he is gone, we still think of him as he was when he was here. It was probably one of the few times that Scott had been forced to think of him as a corpse, buried in that hallowed ground just beneath our feet. I could feel the morbidity of it float into the air.

Oddly enough, at the base of Jason's stone was a photo that I had left during my August visit. I would always take at least one photo that I had laminated and leave it by the stone. I had left it in the grass, leaning into the marble. It was quite windy that day and I remember thinking that it would probably blow away before I had even returned to the car. Yet, here it was all these weeks later. It was one of the photos of Jason in Iraq that we had gotten off of a disposable camera that he had sent home a few weeks before his death. It was one of the few photos of him there that showed a smile that we recognized. I think the most difficult aspect of the whole visitation for Scott was having walked upon that grave only to see Jason smiling at him.

We returned to the car for the others and prepared all the things we had brought for our "party." We went back to the grave together and lovingly placed our objects in carefully calculated positions. We put a flower vase into the ground first, just beside the stone. We had chosen vibrant orange and purple daisies with yellow and red carnations. Jason would have loved both the colors and the simplicity of the flowers. Courtland and Carter were disappointed that wild mustard was no longer in bloom, but were satisfied with this common flora. Next we placed some laminated photos that I had taped to Popsicle sticks into the ground in front of the stone. The pictures were Courtland and Carter's school pictures, my favorite photo of Jason and myself taken at my sister's wedding, a close up of Jason in his favorite cowboy hat and best of all was a larger picture of Jason playing with the Iraqi children. This picture came to us in a disposable camera that was in with his effects sent back from Iraq. What a blessing. That picture of him playing with the children showed Jason doing what he loved. It shows a smile more like what we were accustomed to and the last one of these we would ever see. Only the joy of a child could have brought that to him so far away from home. It is our reminder of what he fought for. That one picture simply defined Jason.

Next, we propped an old cowboy hat up against the flowers and one of Carter's old, totally worn out, cowboy boots up against the other side of the stone. I could almost hear Jason laughing. He would have loved knowing that while most kids Carter's age grow out of their shoes, Carter wore his out. This was because his boots rarely left his feet. Other shoes were seldom an option and never without stern pressure from Mom. I'm not certain, but it's possible he was born wearing boots and come to think of it, spurs could explain a lot. Jason had received his first pair when he was four years old and was never without a pair until the day he died. None of his boots ever survived to be passed along either, not until his death. He would have been honored to see the sad condition of this chunk of Carter's worn leather and would have been certain that it was due to his excellent brotherly genetics. Justin had always preferred boots, although never insisted on colors like fire engine red and at least had sense enough to take them off at night, most of the time. Courtland, being my most unique creation, had waited until he ceased to be marveled by the magic of Velcro before he decided he wanted a pair of boots.

We had a tiny birthday cake that I think Courtland had a hard time giving up. I promised him one for us all to share at home on Monday, Jason's actual birthday, and he relented. We had wax numbers that said '20' for the top. We also had a bottle of Sparking Cider. Justin and Jason loved to have this for Thanksgiving dinner, a tradition started at my mother-in-laws when they were just little. They felt so grown up because the bottle looked like something for adults only. Jason never ceased to be thrilled when I'd pick some up for a family meal anytime after that and had been keeping this particular bottle in his room for a special occasion. While he had long since discovered what adult beverage was all about; this special memory of his childhood was still held dear. It just seemed like this would be a good time to break it out. We tied a few helium balloons to the bottle and while some people choose to leave stones behind on a cemetery marker, we went with farm animals. Jason was always known for having miniature farm animals in his pockets. First, they were for him to play with and later for any children he may come across. We set up two little horses that resembled his real horses, Punk and Prince, and Courtland added a dairy cow for good measure. After we were finished, we admired our handiwork and quietly sang, "Happy Birthday to You." The children sang with vigor, as if to lift the words and melody right up to the Heavens so Jason could hear. Never had they meant them more. I did well for about two bars and then started breaking. My mother, who had been trying so hard to keep it together for the boys, as well as me, was pushing back tears as hard as she could. She sang weakly, but she sang. Scott had been forced to retreat to the car and we let him have the privacy he needed. He could see and hear us from where he was and I knew that the words were passing over his lips too. At the end of our tune, the boys released exactly twenty helium filled balloons into the air. We watched them float upward toward Heaven, taking their time to flint about and dance and the world around us seemed to mute itself as we stood there watching them diminish in size. I told the children that I was going to pretend that Jason would reach down out of Heaven and snatch them up just as they floated out of our sight and that he would share them with the angels as they celebrated his birthday there. They seemed to think this perfectly reasonable and acceptable.

We stayed for a little while longer and when we all agreed that we were ready, we headed back to the car. Scott and I squeezed one another's hands and we drove onward in silence. I would not look back today. I could not leave my baby behind today, on his birthday. If I didn't look back I could try to pretend it wasn't so.

I could tell Scott was going to take the scenic way out and thought that was exactly what we could use. Just as we had made our first turn into another section of the cemetery, we were all startled to see something foreign and completely out of place. There, dancing a delicate ballet of grace and serenity were four deer. They casually glanced up, quite undisturbed by our presence and if I didn't absolutely know better, I would have sworn they smiled. There were two enormous bucks, a doe and a younger buck. They seemed to be in harmony with the holiness of this place. I have no idea where they came from but their celestial aura seemed such a stark contrast to the cement jungle that lay not a stone's throw away from this place. I think their presence meant something a little different to each of us but we all seemed to agree that we had found sufficient evidence that the balloons had indeed been well received.

After being so inspired, we decided not to leave the cemetery immediately, but to take a little time and tour some of the other notable resting-places. We ended up visiting John F. Kennedy's gravesite next. The children had not yet been there. They were so proud to see the wall where the famous words that Kennedy had spoken and Jason had quoted in his senior yearbook were inscribed. "Ask not what your country can do for you..." They were not at all sure that Jason should not also have an eternal flame. After all, did he not share the same philosophy and live his life accordingly? Certainly he was no less important. Carter surmised that it must simply be a matter of being the first to say something great. After all, who could argue with "getting dibs?" Since JFK was born so much earlier, he obviously got credit for "calling it." They then shifted their attention to the two tiny graves on either side of John and Jackie. They were very saddened to learn that the Kennedy's had two children that had not lived and in sympathy for such a great tragedy decided that the flame could remain with them.

We went to the Tomb of the Unknown Soldier next. They had been schooled on all the symbolism of this site and had just seen on Friday's newscast Vice President Cheney participating in the wreath laying ceremony for Veterans Day. They carefully counted each of the guard's twenty-one steps and then counted the twenty-one seconds, under their breath, each time he paused. The changing of the guard ceremony mesmerized them and just before we left we were even able to see an entire wreath laying ceremony.

Emotionally spent and hungry, we loaded up to leave Arlington. Though near an exit already, Scott decided to drive past where Jason lay one more time. I guess it was his way of saying bye. I thought I had made the break without imploding. Now, here we were again. I was trying desperately. Just one more glimpse.

We were making the pass. I was tracking. Suddenly the car stopped and Scott got out. He promised a speedy return and then went to the grave one last time. Good-byes never came easy, no matter how accustomed to them we believed ourselves to have become.

Even with our best efforts that day, we all drove away with our hands on the glass reaching back for the child we wrongly left behind.

The ride home seemed like an eternity. We stopped for a lovely dinner in which the food was tasty, the conversation was enjoyable and we were all left with full bellies. Why then, must we still feel so empty? We drove on into the night, sometimes in silence but always subdued. When we finally walked into our home the emptiness engulfed us and seemingly took our collective breath. The children felt it in their own way as well, although they had no words to describe it or any ability to comprehend it. I just knew that they had been swept up in it as well by the expressions on their faces and their hesitation at moving inside any further. Being resilient like children are, they quickly regrouped and ran off together to burn off some of their pent up energy. Scott and I quietly dropped ourselves into chairs in different rooms. What was there to say? Neither of us had anything left. There were no more words. There was no energy left to try to find new ones. We were too numb to even try to reach out to each other. We couldn't have felt it anyway. There was just sadness. Sadness and emptiness. More mourning. Grief had taken a new life form today. We left the pieces of the corpse one hundred and fifty miles away and came home to the emptiness of the child no longer here.   Everything that was Jason had been visited upon us today.   It was as though we had taken Ebenezer Scrooge's midnight journey but instead of waking up to a beautiful Christmas full of hope, we were damned to return to his chamber of doom.   His life. His death. His eternity.   Where did that leave us?   What did that leave us?

After a time in silence, Scott asked how I was doing.   I gave the standard response and posed the same question to him.   He replied in kind and we both knew we were liars.   There was at least some strange comfort in that.   He went to bed shortly afterward.   I knew he was exhausted and yet I heard the television upstairs. He couldn't be with anyone, yet he couldn't be alone.   I understood that particular misery all too well.

I went in to talk to the children about our day and we decided that it was overall a good one.   They thought we had chosen a fine way to mark the passing of Jason's would be birthday.   They had felt sadness but had also felt pride and honor.   They missed him terribly but felt as close as they could, knowing he was never coming home.   I kissed them and tucked them into bed and reminded them how proud of them I was.   We said the "now I lay me down to sleep" prayer and Carter wanted to know if Jason heard our prayers too.   I assured him that he did and he seemed convinced that he suddenly stood a much better chance of having certain ones answered.   I wondered if he had been asking God to pony up some new cowboy boots.

I turned off the lights and thought how strange it was that I was the one winding up the day downstairs while Scott was in bed.   It had been the other way for what seemed like such a long time.   He had done everything while I had fallen apart and tonight I was the keeper of the flame while he did.   It reminded me of a story that Dr. Phil often told about a man who was asked the secret of his long, successful marriage.   The man replied that luckily, he and his wife had never fallen out of love at the same time.   Luckily for us, Scott and I had simply not yet fallen at the same time.

"Now I lay me down to sleep.... please, God, let our luck hold out."

CHAPTER 17

ABSOLUTION

As I continued to grow into the woman I was becoming, I was still bothered by the fact that I had yet to reestablish certain relationships in my life. My mother was a huge issue for me.

One of the members of my grief group was talking about having a conversation with her mother and discovering how much her mother had suffered just in watching her. O.K., Oprah, here is my lightbulb moment.

I knew how much my mother loved Jason and I had only thought of her loss in those terms. I had actually felt horrible on many occasions as she was left alone to fall in line as best she could. I wanted nothing more than to fall into her arms and stay there, yet to do so would surely mean it was all real and that may be a place I could never rise up from. I was terrified of seeing her fall apart. She had ALWAYS been steel to me. If she were to crumble it would all be real. It was imperative that we both maintain our stations to keep this wolf at bay. It remains that way today.

I began to think after that meeting about what it must be like for her to see her daughter flounder as I have. I know she has been proud of me on many occasions since Jason left us. Was this because at those moments she could see me, still, in there somewhere? Was she hopeful at these moments that I would survive this? I have writhed in pain knowing what my sons were suffering and feeling like I was powerless to heal them. I finally surmised that she, too, knew this for me.

I have not yet been able to talk to my sister. She is drowning in her own grief and I am terrified she will pull me under. I must maintain my level of denial to stay buoyant. She is fording through the tough stuff and just trying to deal with the reality daily. I have to just pretend sometimes that this has not been a part of our lives. If I don't, I would never be able to grasp the beauty of the present. I may not even be able to exist in it. Therefore, answering the phone would mean certain sinking for me. She knows I love her and cannot understand why I am so withdrawn. I'm sorry, Rita. Maybe the new me will float well enough one-day to talk to you about it. I do love you.

It wasn't just with relationships I had known from birth. My friend, Rebecca, had been as close to me as a sister. We would argue about money, education, child rearing, dogs, politics, religion and the world in general. She was also one person who would whip the butt of anybody that had anything negative to say about me. She LOVED Jason. He had dated her daughter on and off and had loved her since he was old enough to feel that little pitty pat in the heart that one gets for a girl for the first time. (or so I'm told!) He told everyone that eventually they would both grow up and that he and Tarah would spend their lives together. I am quite certain that had he made it home, it would have been her doorstep his boots would have first crossed.

Rebecca and her husband, Tony, had become so accustomed to Jason's presence, that even when the kids were spatting, Jason remained a fixture in their home. He even had his own Christmas stocking that was put up every year regardless of whom Tarah was dating at the time. Rebecca placed that same stocking in his casket.

Jason always took new girlfriends to Tony and Rebecca's for dinner and approval. They would always give him a grade on each based on their perception of whether or not they believed the young lady in question could make him as happy as their "son" deserved to be.

They had watched him grow into a man and they loved him deeply. I loved them deeply. Rebecca, along with Avis, was responsible for finding clothes for me when Jason died. I think she must have purchased every pair of Queen (even fat chicks like to be referred to in a royal manner–it's much better than Size Chubby) Subtle Shapers pantyhose that J.C.Penney had in stock before it was all over.   I just kept losing them.   I'm sure the cashier must have wondered what she was doing buying twenty pairs of pantyhose that were four sizes too big for her!   They were tasteful enough not to ask.

Rebecca was always the one I would call on to drive me to Arlington.   I'll never forget the time we went into the cemetery through Fort Myer Army base and the gate guard asked us where we were headed.   Rebecca simply said, "Jason's grave."   The guard repeated it and let us through as though we had just said "Kennedy's grave."   I seemed to be the only one that thought this unusual.

All of that connection.   All of that comfort.   Yet, she was my one friend I couldn't call and talk to about it now. Too much time had passed, emotionally speaking.   Was I afraid of taking her back to that place or was I afraid she would take me?   I didn't know but she would be part of my new three pronged attack to clear up these areas in my life: MOTHER, SISTER, NON-RELATED SISTER. Maybe not in that order.

During this time of reconstruction, I received a card from a chaplain in California.   He had corresponded with me many times since Jason's death and always seemed to know when I needed a little encouragement.

He had met Jason while the group from Camp LeJeune was in California waiting final deployment to Iraq. Chaplain Presley had been counseling the young Marines during their two-week stay.   Jason had apparently been one of these young men.

When Chaplain Presley would write me, he would speak of Jason with such familiarity.   He seemed to be feeling such a personal loss and I wondered many times how it was that he remembered Jason so vividly.   He must have visited with thousands of men.

Upon reading this latest card, I decided to write him and finally ask that very question.   I had also been very disturbed by something since I became aware that Jason had visited with him so often.   I decided to dump this on Chaplain Presley.   I figured this sort of thing was his field and it was weighing heavy on my heart.   I had shared this burden with no one. I guess I was hoping that in somehow engaging in a confession, he might throw a Hail Mary or two my way and even though I am not Catholic, it could stick.

I told him that I had been burdened by guilt because I had not flown to California to see Jason one last time before he flew off to Iraq. I thought that since he had specifically sought out the chaplain's counsel so often that he must have been very alone and frightened. I could picture it in my mind's eye and I hated myself for not going to him. I should have known that even though he told me differently on the phone, that of course, he was scared.

His response came on a day when I had been finding my struggle all uphill. I trembled a little as I clicked on the email.

'DEAR RHONDA.

I AM BLESSED THAT YOU WROTE.

GOD DREW ME TO JASON. HE RADIATED LIGHT AND SALT OF CHRIST IN THAT WONDERFUL SMILE. I CAN STILL PICTURE HIM SITTING THERE WITH HIS BUDDIES, JAMEL DANIELS AND DAVID GERONDAKIS. IT WAS NOT ONLY HIS SMILE BUT HE MODELED CHRIST BEING CONCERNED MORE FOR OTHERS THAN HIMSELF.

THESE QUALITIES AND THEN FURTHER LEARNING ABOUT THE IMPACT HE MADE ON THE YOUNG PEOPLE AT HIS SCHOOL...HIS LEGACY WILL LIVE ON FOR YEARS TO COME AND IT WILL BEAR FRUIT. THE IMPACT HE MADE ON IRAQI CHILDREN HE WOULD DISTRIBUTE CANDY TO; THAT IS TRULY HOW TERRORISM IS GOING TO BE DEFEATED THROUGH REACHING THOSE CHILDREN WITH LOVE.

I OFTEN USE JASON AS AN ILLUSTRATION OF WHAT A HEROIC MARINE LOOKS LIKE SERVING IN THE STRENGTH OF CHRIST. HE COULD HAVE OPTED OUT BY EITHER NOT GOING ON THAT MISSION OR ENTIRELY BY TRANSFERRING TO THE HONOR GUARD.

*I CAN HONESTLY TELL YOU THAT I DID NOT SENSE
FEAR AT ALL FROM HIM BUT COURAGEOUS RESOLVE
AND HE HAD THE PEACE OF CHRIST BEFORE HE
BOARDED THAT PLANE ON JULY 6, 2004. I HAVE A
STRONG RELATIONSHIP WITH HIS COMMANDING
OFFICER, MAJOR BILLY MOORE AND FIRST SERGEANT
WOOTTEN, WHO INDICATED HE WAS AN IMPACT
MARINE-ONE WHO HONORED THE UNIFORM HE WORE.
AS A MATTER OF FACT, WE AGAIN ARE PRAYING FOR
THE 1 / 2 AS THEY HAVE RETURNED TO IRAQ. BE AT
PEACE, SISTER. WHAT I SAW WAS A MAN, A MARINE
WHO WAS RESOLVED HE HAD A JOB TO DO AND HIS
FRIENDS DREW ON HIS COURAGE. IT WAS NOT
BRAVADO, IT WAS CHRIST.*

*HE EXEMPLIFIED CHRIST WHEN I ASKED HIM WHAT I
NEEDED TO PRAY FOR HIM. HE SAID HE WOULD
WANT PRAYER FOR YOU, THAT YOU WOULD BE CARED
FOR AND NOT WORRY.*

*IT IS GOD'S WILL THAT I REMEMBER HIM AS VIVIDLY
BECAUSE HE REMINDS ME OF THE VERSE IN
COLOSSIANS TO DWELL ON WHAT IS GOOD, WHAT IS
HONORABLE, WHAT IS BEAUTIFUL. IN THE MIDST OF
THIS CONFLICT, I REMEMBER JASON AND THAT HOPE
THAT HE STOOD FOR...THAT HOPE IS IN CHRIST. HIS
BROTHERS AND HIS FAMILY WILL HAVE A GOOD
EXAMPLE TO FOLLOW AND ONE DAY WE WILL ALL BE
UNITED AGAIN WITH HIM WHO KNOW CHRIST."*

Oh, I thought it was something like that. PLEASE! Man,
talk about your, "ask and ye shall receive"!
SHAZAM!!!!

I was so pleased with my newfound enlightenment. I
began to think that we would somehow survive the
upcoming holidays.

I had made a decision soon after Jason's death that I
would not be home for Christmas. I felt the offensive
approach would be best. After all, NOBODY wants to
deal with the "first " Christmas. So, I began tentatively
planning. I ran through several ideas and honestly
thought for quite some time that Scott would not be able

to go with me. This presented a whole different conundrum. I didn't think I could face Christmas at home this year but I certainly didn't think I wanted to face it anywhere without my husband. I forged ahead anyway with my newfound optimism, hoping for a miracle.

Scott, at first, was panicked wondering how he was supposed to get away and then slowly he began to resign himself into somehow making it work. He was the one that suggested Disney World and though I was afraid he had turned to smoking crack, I jumped all over the idea.

During the next several weeks, Scott came to me and announced that he was going to sell the dairy cows. He said that since Jason wasn't coming home he had no more reason to keep fighting it. He held on hoping that if Jason came home and was struggling with finding out who he now was, that he would have a focus and a purpose for him to use as long as he needed. He knew how much Jason loved the farm and thought they could have a little business together if Jason wanted. Scott didn't know how much Jason would be able to do, but it didn't matter. Of course, he hoped that after a few months home Jason would be able to find his way and move on with the life that he planned for himself. As we listened to him moving further and further away in those last phone calls and we saw that emailed photo of his face, Scott decided he would do what he could to have a backup plan in place for him. Jason would have dutifully served his country and it would be just fine if he never ventured off the farm again.

Scott was now left with a plan and no one to enact it. He was lost in a way I never imagined possible. How could I have been married to this man for so long and still find myself at a place where I didn't know him?

I watched him begin to drift. The farm had been his life. How many holidays had the children and I spent basically without him? How many vacations had we gone on alone? Seven days a week those cows needed to be cared for and while I'm sure they were all very sorry to keep the kids waiting on Christmas morning, they unfortunately still needed to be milked and fed.

We were all aware of the benefits of farm life and none of us wanted to give those up so we learned to make it all work. This is what Scott had grown up doing. This is what he went to college for. This is what he would do for a living the rest of his life. He loved his work, most of the time, and never saw a different future, until now.

Scott knew, as I did, that the holidays would be difficult at best. I think the final straw was having to think about Christmas morning in the parlor, alone. The Christmas before was without Jason as well because he was in Iraq. That was hard enough and at that time we still believed he would be home in a few weeks. This was different. He would never know another Christmas morning in that barn. I just think that was more reality than he cared to have settle over him.

This had been Scott's life and what he believed would be his future. This was now going to be another ending.

He did sell the herd. The closing was on a Friday and we left Saturday, Christmas Eve morning for Disney World! We were taking Scott's granddads' camper and were spending Christmas in Orlando.

I had thought many times during the last weeks leading up to Christmas that if I did not have this trip to look forward to that I just would not be able to make it. I wanted desperately to give Courtland and Carter a holiday without a death cloud hanging over it. I imagined us laughing together and sharing genuine joy. I didn't even think I could open our ornament box, much less put up the tree. This alternate plan would let us have an adventure to look forward to. I bought a little artificial tree for the camper and the boys picked out some cheap ornaments and we were set. We were NOT sliding headfirst into the holiday pit. We were going to see Mickey.

We took reindeer food so Santa would be able to find us and we decorated the outside of the camper in the tackiest manner we could think of once we arrived. God bless an Airstream illuminated with giant multi-colored Christmas bulbs!

We found beautiful weather there and the entire vacation could not have been more perfect. Courtland actually looked up at me during the fireworks at Disney World and said, "This really is the most magical place on Earth!"

We collapsed in our beds at night and jumped up before the sun every morning. Everything in between was bliss. We had the best Christmas the children had ever known. Christmas morning in that little camper was the greatest Christmas present I had ever received.

We were on our way into the stadium at Sea World one evening when my cell phone rang. It was Justin. Missy was in labor. How rude! I couldn't believe they weren't waiting for me to get home. We had almost four weeks left! I told him to stay calm, give Missy our love and to keep me posted.

As I walked in to see Shamu, I realized that very soon I would be a grandma.

Jasmine Skye Redifer was born on December 30, 2005. They were headed home from the hospital the same day we were headed home from Florida. I met her the following morning and welcomed her to the world. She was our new beginning.

CHAPTER 18

AROUND THE SUN

Lynn Mitchell emailed me the night of January 30, 2006 and told me that she was working on a memorial message for the one-year anniversary of Jason's death. She was sending it out on the Staunton, Waynesboro, Augusta County (SWAC) Newsletter. This was the information "go to" spot for the area Republicans. She was dedicating an entire edition that would run the following day. She offered me an open forum to say anything that was on my mind.

I certainly appreciated the opportunity to somehow address those that had supported me so greatly, yet what was there left to say?

I was feeling the gravity of the anniversary bearing down on me and was just too distraught to even think. I left the computer, already crying, and went into Jason's room.

You never really know what to expect there. Sometimes it is a place that will absolutely take you down and sometimes I find great comfort there. I decided to roll the dice and see what I would get.

I sat in his favorite chair, one that I had physically drug out to the farm dumpster once only to find it back inside by dinner time. Jason was furious that I had tried to dispose of the "most comfortable chair he had ever sat in!" It became the piece the entire bedroom was "built" around. This meant it caught everything from book bags to cowboy boots and still managed to have enough room for him.

I smiled remembering these things and looked around the room. Now filled with letters, photos, awards, mementos, etc., there was barely an empty space. Yet, the entire room was an empty space because Jason wasn't in it. This area now housed all of the things that were there originally (except his bed, which was in another room now,) as well as the hundreds of things we had been given since his death. It was all about Jason and sometimes I actually felt his presence there with me. I just wished he could come home to see all of the wonderful things people had given him.

I had been keeping everything I could get my hands on that related to him and had hundreds of pages in notebooks so I could thumb through things when I was lonely. I picked up one of these notebooks and began flipping through.

I landed right on a copy of an article I had written shortly after Jason's death for a magazine called *The Virginia Dairyman*. The gentleman who was usually responsible for such things for the magazine had a son serving in Iraq and he was scheduled to come home soon. It just hit too close for him and I was asked to submit something, if possible. The article was printed with two of my favorite pictures of Jason, one in his cowboy hat and the other kneeling and playing with the children in Iraq. The article read:

"Although growing up on a dairy farm in the Shenandoah Valley didn't provide him with privilege or wealth, it did provide him with a strong sense of God and country. Marine Lance Corporal Jason C. Redifer was raised by his mother and stepfather along with three brothers on Twin Springs Farm in Stuarts Draft, VA.

As with most farm children, Jason developed an important work ethic early on. He learned what responsibility and accountability meant and expected both from those around him. The children learned to believe that "the Lord giveth and the Lord taketh away" and blessings were to be found in both.

Jason and his older brother Justin learned to value an education as well. When the boys were old enough to attend high school, they both worked several jobs to supplement the financial aid offered enabling them to both attend private schools. Justin attended a military academy while Jason decided to forge his own pathway through academics at a formerly all-girls school. He always understood the important balance of work and play.

Both brothers felt that as Americans they had an obligation to serve their country at some point and the events of September 11, 2001 cemented that for both of them. Justin joined the Army as a military policeman and has worked his way to the rank of Sergeant. Jason left for boot camp at Parris Island just three days after graduation at only seventeen years of age. Everyone was disappointed that the boys had chosen to postpone college but their pride and enthusiasm for their country was contagious.

The gravity of those decisions hit home in July of 2004 when Jason was deployed to Iraq. As his family members gathered to send him off, they one by one said their good-byes. This would be the last time they would ever see him. His stepfather was wondering if he had told him enough how much he loved him and how proud of him he was. Had he given him all the life's lessons that he would need? His older brother was obviously feeling guilt because he was not the one going. His two younger brothers just could not understand why their "superhero" was headed off into the world without them. Lastly, his mother knew she may never hold her child in her arms again and wondered how she would go on if she could not. Jason could almost not bear leaving his family behind but he firmly believed, as President Bush had suggested, that this war on terrorism must be addressed on the enemy's soil rather than ours. He was perfectly willing to lay his life down if it possibly meant that this war was kept from the doorstep of his family.

Jason was very aware of the fact that there were many Americans, who condemned what he was doing, many who disparaged our flag and many who refused to support his Commander In Chief. He was also very aware that it was his job to ensure that those people were continued the freedom to feel that way. Jason, unlike his brother, was not married. He also had no children to leave behind and therefore believed this made him the obvious person to go. While there were often *times he questioned the progress of the war and wondered about the overall outcome, he knew that as long as we are fighting under the banner of freedom against the proponents of tyranny, then our work is not unjust.*

Jason lived long enough to know that the Iraqi elections were deemed a success and to know that he played an important part in that. He spoke of that with pride in an early morning telephone call with his mother just one day later. Jason was heading out on his final patrol mission in Iraq when the Humvee he was traveling in was destroyed by an improvised explosive device. He was killed instantly–just nine days before he was scheduled to leave Iraq and just two hours after the phone call with his mom.

While words could never express the loss that the family is feeling, there is some comfort in knowing that Jason died doing what he believed in for those he loved. Many people are forced to say a final farewell to loved ones everyday. We most always feel it is too soon. There are few situations, however, in which the loved one leaves us with such honor. We truly believe that everyone that ever-encountered Jason, both here and abroad, are better for having met him. After all, "the Lord giveth and the Lord taketh away" and we must find blessings in both."

I sat there for a long time afterward thinking about all of the blessings that I had been given. I had thought of them from time to time as "consolation prizes." They were little gifts from God that reminded us that He was still there and had not forgotten about our struggle or our pain. He had not taken his leave.

I was so blessed that my marriage had not only survived our loss but had been fortified by it. We had been as naked and as raw as humans ever will be and in our vulnerability we had found shelter and a trust within each other like we had never known. I had a new relationship with Justin, far beyond a mother and a son. We had become lifelines for one another. He and Missy (whom I loved as my own) had just welcomed this wonderful, beautiful, new baby girl into their lives. I, of course, had become all about pink! It was totally foreign to me but was an area that I was happy to pursue. I regretted so much that Jason had not had the opportunity to hold and love this little slice of Heaven but I know he is just over her tiny little shoulder. How lucky she will be! I swear I hear him laughing every time Justin changes a diaper or laments about the cost of formula!

I needed this little reminder as I was running headlong into this anniversary that I had been dreading. I knew now exactly what I needed to say, both to myself and to our friends that would be reading the SWAC newsletter.

I got up (after struggling violently with that wretched chair) and headed for my computer. I smiled at Jason's picture on the way out and mouthed, "thank you, Son."

I made myself comfortable and began writing:

"As I prepare to face the anniversary of Jason's passing, I am uncertain as to what I should feel. I once wrote an article describing the events of the past year and I remember saying that "the Lord giveth and the Lord taketh away, and we must find blessings in both." I suppose that is where I am today. The 31st will in many ways be just day number 365 of this place where I have been thrust into. Jason will be no more dead or no less dead. I suppose it will be a time where I will allow myself to stop pretending that it never happened and that he is still just deployed, and force myself to sit down and just let the gravity of it all wash over me. Sometimes it is important to just be with your own reality. I will tell myself that I have now officially made it once around the calendar and that no matter what comes now, I have survived each of these dreadful days at least once.

So, if the worst is no worse, then I'll try to turn myself toward what is better. I have never been more aware of God's blessings than in this past year. Ironically, in my greatest sorrow and loss I have found gifts beyond any I had ever known. I have been blessed with people in my life that have comforted me, carried me, and sustained me. Some were longtime friends, some were new acquaintances, and all were miracles. Those of you reading this must know that you are in this group. I have been delivered from the rubble of my broken soul by your loving words, prayers, cards, calls, hugs and even your very thoughts. You supported me while my heart attempted to mend and kept my family and me close to your breast where I can hear what a perfect heart sounds like.

Thank you all for your devotion to my family, your commitment to our troops so valiantly fighting for our freedom, your support of our President and those who so faithfully serve us, and your unwavering pride in our country and all who fly her flag. May God bless you all and may he continue to bless America.

I am humbly,
Rhonda Winfield"

Enough said.

Editor's note: Rhonda and her family did return to Camp Lejeune in April 2006. They joined hundreds of other family members from the cities of the North, towns and plains of the Mid-West, farmlands of the South and the far West, for a Second Division Memorial Service held for her son Jason and his fellow Marines who fell in the fight against terrorism. They stared at 265 displays of rifles, boots and helmets overlooking the serene blue sea off Camp Lejeune. On a beautiful spring day they came to remember the sacrifices their loved ones had made during the past year in Iraq.

Major General Richard A. Huck, Second Marine Division commanding general, told the audience, "These Marines, Soldiers and Sailors are our friends. They were high school athletes, college students, the kid next door. But they each volunteered to serve and give something bigger than themselves ... It is said that every Marine who ever lived is living still in the Marines that claim the title today. This is the essence of being a Marine. May they remain forever living in your memory... they will in ours."